Mr Midshipman VC

For Marnie
and
In memory of Jack Sillery

Mr Midshipman VC

The Short Accident-Prone Life of George Drewry, Gallipoli Hero

Quentin Falk

Pen & Sword
MARITIME

First published in Great Britain in 2018
by Pen & Sword Maritime
An imprint of Pen & Sword Books Limited
47 Church Street
Barnsley
South Yorkshire
S70 2AS

Copyright © Quentin Falk 2018

ISBN 978 1 52672 624 7

The right of Quentin Falk to be identified as
Author of this Work has been asserted by him in accordance
with the Copyright, Designs and Patents Act 1988.

A CIP catalogue record for this book is
available from the British Library

Typeset in Ehrhardt
by Mac Style

Printed and bound in the UK
by TJ International Ltd, Padstow, Cornwall

Pen & Sword Books Limited incorporates the imprints of Atlas,
Archaeology, Aviation, Discovery, Family History, Fiction, History,
Maritime, Military, Military Classics, Politics, Select, Transport,
True Crime, Air World, Frontline Publishing, Leo Cooper,
Remember When, Seaforth Publishing, The Praetorian Press,
Wharncliffe Local History, Wharncliffe Transport,
Wharncliffe True Crime and White Owl.

For a complete list of Pen & Sword titles please contact
PEN & SWORD BOOKS LIMITED
47 Church Street, Barnsley, South Yorkshire, S70 2AS, England
E-mail: enquiries@pen-and-sword.co.uk
Website: www. pen-and-sword.co.uk

Contents

List of Illustrations		vi
Introduction and Acknowledgments		viii
Chapter 1	V Beach, 25 April (am)	1
Chapter 2	North and South	11
Chapter 3	On the Ocean Wave	19
Chapter 4	V Beach, 25 April (contd.)	34
Chapter 5	For Valour	52
Chapter 6	Suvla Bay: from 10am, 6 August	75
Chapter 7	Suvla Bay, from 6am, 7 August – 2am, 9 August	86
Chapter 8	Suvla Bay: From 2am, 9 August – 1.30pm, 12 August	95
Chapter 9	A Family at War	105
Chapter 10	On Active Service	117
Chapter 11	'Life's work well done'	127
Appendix I: Stories from Real Life: Melbourne Argus, *28 April 1937*		143
Appendix II: Living with the Legacy		147
Sources/Bibliography		152
Index		155

List of Illustrations

The four Drewry brothers in 1901: l-r: Percy, 11, Harry, 13, Ralph, 4, and George, 7. (*Heather Thorne*)

Drewry family photo 1908: l-r: Harry, George, Thomas, Mary Ann, Ralph and Percy. (*Heather Thorne*)

George (right) with oldest brother, Harry. (*Heather Thorne*)

53 Kitchener (formerly Haslemere) Road, Forest Gate. (*Quentin Falk*)

58 Claremont Road, Forest Gate. (*Quentin Falk*)

The ships of George Drewry: SV *Indian Empire* (© *Wrecksite.com*); SS *Isis* (© *P&O Heritage Collection*); HMS *Hussar* (© *Imperial War Museum*); HMS *Conqueror* (© MOD, Naval Historical Branch); HMT *William Jackson* (after being renamed SV *Evelyn Rose*). (*Bernard McCall*)

The *River Clyde* approaching V Beach. (*Stephen Chambers*)

V Beach, today and, inset, April 1915. (*Quentin Falk* / © *Imperial War Museum*.

Map of Cape Helles. (*John Fawkes*)

George (head bandaged) with Dr Peter Burrowes Kelly after V Beach landing. (*Central News*)

Map of Suvla Bay. (*John Fawkes*)

View of A Beach, Suvla Bay, 2018. (*Quentin Falk*) / Landing at A Beach, August 1915. (*Norman Wilkinson*)

Three 'middies' on Imbros, August 1915. Officially captioned: l-r: George, Wilfred Malleson, Greg Russell. More likely – Russell, Malleson, and Drewry. (© *Imperial War Museum*)

Among the crew with HMS *Hussar* officers, autumn 1916: top row – l-r: Hewetson, Moore, Burton, Ellis; middle row: l-r: Giffard,

Heneage, Hennessey; front row: l-r: George, Simeon, Fletcher. (*Heather Thorne*)

George (right) off duty with fellow officers on Imbros. (© *Imperial War Museum*)

At the palace for his investiture, November 1916: l-r, Ralph (left) and George with their mother Mary Ann. (© *Imperial War Museum*)

Daily Sketch front page, November 22. (*John Frost Newspapers / Alamy Stock Photo*)

Scapa Flow, 2018 and, inset, during the Great War. (*Angus Konstam / Orkney Library and Archive*)

Portrait of a VC. (*Heather Thorne*)

Last photo of George at the rail of HMT *William Jackson*, August 1918. (*George T. Drewry*)

George's body is horse-drawn into the City of London Cemetery, 10 August 1918. (© *Imperial War Museum*)

George's grave at the City of London Cemetery. (*Richard Tedham*)

George's Sword of Honour presented by the Imperial Merchant Service Guild. (© *Imperial War Museum*)

Memorial window to George at All Saints Church, Forest Gate. (*Richard Tedham*)

'The VC Middies' of the Dardanelles. (*Boy's Own Paper*)

George (foreground) with bandaged head during his VC action as featured in 'Deeds that Thrilled an Empire: Vol 1'. (© *N&M Press*)

George in action. (*War Budget*)

Cartoon from *The Bulletin*, 18 August 1915. (*Heather Thorne*)

Detail of the hopper *Argyle* in the 1938 diorama of the V Beach landing. (© *Imperial War Museum*)

Front and back cover of *The Hornet*, 5 November 1966. (© *DC Thomson & Co Ltd*)

George T. Drewry, George's oldest surviving nephew. (*Quentin Falk*)

Centenary commemorative stone to George in Central Park, East Ham. (*Richard Tedham*)

The author at Suvla Bay. (*John Mackenzie*)

Introduction and Acknowledgments

When I arrived for the first time on the peninsula in May 2012, my knowledge of the ill-fated Dardanelles campaign was principally informed by repeated viewings down the years of *Gallipoli*, Peter Weir's beautifully crafted and movingly acted, if highly sentimentalized, Anzac version of events which was released to deserved acclaim in 1981.

Coincidentally, I happened to be in South Australia during its much-anticipated production and, although some scenes of pre-battle training were filmed in Egypt, the blood-spattered beaches, gullies and ravines of 1915 were actually recreated about 400 miles from Adelaide, by the seaside and on the cliffs in and around Port Lincoln, including a cove that has now been re-named Gallipoli Beach.

However, while the actual authenticity of Weir's rather fine film is perhaps a little dubious, the real-life sacrifice of more than 44,000 Allied dead – almost double that on the Turkish side – in an eight-month campaign still remains palpable more than a century after the events.

Among the 22,000 fatalities of the British Empire, excluding Anzacs – which accounted for fully half that number – was my wife's great uncle, Major John Jocelyn Doyne Sillery (known as 'Jack') of the 11th Battalion, Manchester Regiment, who landed at Gallipoli on 6 August. It was a mission to try and find his memorial that had first drawn us to this battlefield tour.

In 1915 the 11th Manchesters were part of 34 Infantry Brigade. On that early August day, a little over three months after the campaign's first amphibious landings had taken place, the 11th embarked on lighters and was towed by destroyers to Suvla Bay, on the west side of the peninsula, about 5 miles beyond Anzac Cove. They grounded 200–300 yards north of Lala Baba, a fortified post held by the Turks at the south of the bay.

The landing was extremely difficult since they were in about 6ft of water, and every man had to be got ashore by means of a rope held by two officers, one on the lighter and one in the water.

According to the Manchester Regiment website: 'Major Sillery landed first in order to collect the men as they came ashore, and other officers were landed at intervals. The landing was carried out under heavy rifle fire from Lala Baba and shrapnel fire from further inland. When the disembarkation had been completed the C.O. found the battalion resting on the beach with bayonets fixed, and ready to move against the ridges to the north of the bay ...'

Some further light is thrown on the individual work of the officers and men of the regiment in a letter from a sergeant major of the battalion, which appeared in *The Ashton Herald* (11 September 1915):

Our division made a new landing. We came in the night, and as soon as we ran the lighters in shore they gave us hell, many men being killed and wounded in the boats. We stuck on a sandbank, and the bullets rained upon us all round. The Colonel called "Tallest men first". I slipped on board, and half-swam and half-waded ashore – a distance of about 200 yards – and was accompanied by the Adjutant and Major Sillery. I was the first man ashore with a rifle. We lay down on the beach, and then started to collect men together as they struggled ashore, and then formed them up.

After a while, and under heavy fire, we managed to get some formation, and fixed bayonets. We then moved off, while bullets still whizzed and shells boomed and burst around us.

Slowly we advanced, wondering how long we could last. After about a mile we got to work, and then the boys proceeded to get their own back, clearing the trenches of Turks with the bayonet. Orders had been given that no shots were to be fired – it was to be all bayonet work …'

Jack Sillery was never seen alive again and he has no known grave. He was mentioned in despatches and is remembered, we were gratified to discover, with honour on the impressive Helles Memorial at the windblown southernmost tip of the peninsula. It takes the form of an obelisk over 30 metres high that can be seen by ships passing through the Dardanelles. He was 48.

Less than a year later, Jack's older brother – my wife's paternal grandfather – Lieutenant Colonel Charles Cecil Archibald Sillery of the 20th (Tyneside Scottish) Battalion, Northumberland Fusiliers, died on 1 July 1916 at the Somme leading his men into battle. He was 54.

Although our priority had initially been family-orientated, it was soon overtaken by an overwhelming sense of a far bigger and bloodier picture, albeit painfully confined to this oddly picturesque killing ground just 48 miles long by 4 miles wide, flanked by the Aegean on one side and the Dardanelles Strait, leading to the Sea of Marmara, on the other.

We'd cross each day to the peninsula by means of a fifteen-minute ferry ride from the bustling seaside town of Canakkale, on the Asia side. Just a 45-minute drive from the ancient Homeric city of Troy, Canakkale also happens to boast, on its 'prom', the giant wooden horse especially recreated for the 2004 film, *Troy*, very loosely based on the *Iliad*.

We walked strenuously, even at times a little hazardously, where troops fought and died a century earlier in mostly foul conditions, ranging from blistering heat to extreme cold as the seasons changed dramatically between April 1915 and January 1916. En route, we were treated to a colourful account of the various actions, which might, in lesser hands, have been rather cool and detached.

However, as illuminated by the estimable Clive Harris, an ex-army man with an infectious grasp of military history, the focus was as much on the human stories, the heroics and the sacrifice, as on the tangled politics, command mismanagement, an insufficient understanding of the terrain, as well as the, sometimes arcane, ordnance detail.

And such stories, individual and ensemble; twelve Victoria Crosses awarded for the very first day of the invasion as Allied troops made their way ashore on to the beaches beneath Cape Helles, most notably on to W Beach – site of the 'Six VCs before breakfast' exploits of the Lancashire Fusiliers – and V Beach, a disembarkation shambles, despite the selfless feats of some Navy men, among them 20-year-old George Leslie Drewry. George had been at sea with the Merchant Marine since the age of 14 before joining the Royal Naval Reserve as a midshipman or 'Snotty'.

As we stood above Ertugrul Cove (officially designated V Beach), at Sedd-el-Bahr, near the Turkish memorial of Yahya Cavus Sehitligi ve Aniti (where the Ottomans counter-attacked that morning), Clive spent perhaps just five minutes or so on Mr Midshipman Drewry, one of six VCs at V Beach. But even in that short time, he painted such a vivid picture of Drewry that it was seared forever into my imagination.

It was of a young man who, after an accident-prone teenage full of unusual, often near fatal, incident, still managed to survive, despite head wounds and the horrors of that last week in April, only to die accidentally – almost tragi-comically in view of what he had already gone through three years earlier – in August, 1918, just a few months shy of the Armistice.

That he also returned to the beaches at Gallipoli as part of the equally disastrous August landings on exactly the same day as Jack Sillery disembarked and then died, only served further to fuel my interest in a fascinating subject, to which now was added an almost spookily serendipitous sense of a genuine family connection.

Over the next four days, as we moved about the scarred terrain, further punctuated here and there with beautifully-maintained cemeteries containing the named and the unknown, Clive told us about other, often equally astonishing, deeds undertaken in places whose quaint-sounding names belied the gory reality. Like The Vineyard, where the 'Cigarette VC', William Forshaw of the 9th Manchesters, lit grenade fuses from his gaspers while chain-smoking for hours on end before hurling them at the attacking Turks; Lone Pine, which yielded no fewer than seven Anzac VCs; and The Tennis Court, where 300 Australians in three desperate waves fell in hours from 4.30am on 7 August – coincidentally the same day Jack Sillery probably died – trying to capture the elusive Nek.

This last, incidentally, was the inspiration for the final assault filmed so dramatically in agonising slow motion for Weir's *Gallipoli*.

I was also touched, as by so many before me, by the sentiments on a large stone memorial high above Anzac Cove, which proclaimed, poignantly, the following:

Those heroes that shed their blood and lost their lives … You are now lying in the soil of a friendly country. Therefore rest in peace. There is no difference between the Johnnies and the Mehmets to us where they lie side by side here in this country of ours … You, the mothers who sent their sons from faraway countries, wipe away your tears; your sons are now lying in our bosom and are in peace. After having lost their lives on this land they have become our sons as well.

It has been attributed – although some now believe, wrongly – to the Turkish commander, Mustafa Kemal, later Ataturk, the founder of modern Turkey.

A little over five years later, I found myself back at Cape Helles, now with a handsomely re-furbished memorial, but this time round I was properly armed, albeit metaphorically, with an almost overwhelming weight of research material – much historically familiar, some, more personal, rather less so – gleaned greedily during the space between my two visits.

Although not a significant element in this particular tale, I began to grasp more fully the significance of the Anzac involvement in the campaign and its enduring legacy; also to understand more about the role of Churchill, who in his role as First Lord of the Admiralty, has consistently been painted a principal villain of the piece.

I was particularly moved reading Jeremy Paxman's *Great Britain's Great War*, which was published during the first year of the centenary, ahead of his BBC TV series on the same subject. Notable were his typically pugnacious reflections on Gallipoli where his great uncle Charlie, of the Royal Army Medical Corps, was killed.

'The levels of incompetence displayed,' he wrote, 'make it hard to consider the entire adventure as anything other than a misguided, irrelevant and costly sideshow which wasted scarce resources and undermined morale. The Dardanelles campaign demonstrated the chasm between the young men who had volunteered to fight the war and the old men who directed it.'

The blame game, I discovered, continues to this day, but what seems to remain indisputable is perhaps best summed up by one of the fiercest contemporary critics of the campaign, British journalist Ellis Ashmead-Bartlett.

In between regularly excoriating the British High Command, its strategy and tactics, both at the time and not long after in his 1928 memoir, unambiguously titled *Uncensored Dardanelles*, he was equally unequivocal about George and his naval fellows that day in April when he wrote, 'Then it was that one of those gallant acts of devotion was performed which brighten the darkest pages of warfare.'

A newish addition to the peninsula, I noted last year, was the impressive Canakkale Epic Promotion Centre, part of a refurbished museum, near the village of Kabatepe. In eleven walk-through galleries, it tells the story, some of it in 3D, of the campaign – known locally as 'The Battle of Canakkale' – albeit from a predominantly Turkish point of view.

Then, on 2 August 2017, exactly 99 years to the day after he died, I was in the Orkneys casting my eyes across the gleaming waters of Scapa Flow under a brilliant blue sky to where George would find his final anchorage. Nowadays large cruise liners rather than the Grand Fleet account for the most significant shipping in those parts.

That George so gallantly shed his blood at Gallipoli yet lived to fight another day only then to lose his life so prosaically away from the immediate heat of battle, and within touching distance of home and peace, seemed at that moment to suggest an almost irresistibly literary, even perversely romantic, ingredient to an already epically tragic tale.

So, as I pondered a suitable title, Captain Frederick Marryat's *Mr Midshipman Easy*, that classic and still oddly timeless pre-Victorian 'Boys' Own' yarn of Royal Naval derring-do, immediately suggested itself, with its convenient nautical parallels and irresistibly similar titular ring.

George's sacrifice among an estimated total of some eighteen million, also brought to mind in this centenary, some words of Hilary Mantel who delivered a recent series of Reith Lectures. She said: 'My concern as a writer is with memory, personal and collective; with the restless dead asserting their claims … giving voice to those who have been silenced.'

George's own 'voice', modest to a fault, is limited here specifically just to four long letters he wrote to his father in 1915 following his involvement at V Beach then Suvla Bay. So my concern was to try and evoke his whole life, not just through his own words, but also through the testimony of fellow combatants as well the remembrance of others.

This notion, in turn, compelled me to re-read Professor Paul Fussell's wonderful *The Great War and Modern Memory*, first published in 1975, which explored, as the distinguished author, a veteran of the Second World War, put it, 'some of the literary means by which it has been remembered, conventionalized and mythologized'.

However, as his influential thesis was strictly limited to the Western Front, I decided that I would attempt an affectionate 'nod' rather than rigorously academic homage to Fussell on behalf of what has sometimes been dismissively termed a 'Great War sideshow'.

Of, in particular, the writers and poets of the Great War, Fussell posed these questions: 'What did the war feel like to those whose world was the trenches? How did they get through this bizarre experience? And finally, how did they transform their feelings into language and literary form?'

So, as well as poring through strictly factual accounts, many dotted with the affecting accounts of eyewitnesses to the unfolding debacle, I also mined some of the fiction and poetry provoked by the campaign. This led me to writers, poets and artists as diverse as A.P. Herbert, John Masefield, Compton Mackenzie, Ernest Raymond, Rachel Billington, Louis de Bernières, Alexander Kent (aka Douglas Reeman), Laurence Binyon, Geoffrey Dearmer, Patrick Shaw-Stewart, Siegfried Sassoon, Michael J. Whelan, Norman Wilkinson and Herbert Hillier, all of whom had either first-hand or familial connections with Gallipoli.

Rupert Brooke, a 27-year-old temporary sub-lieutenant in the Royal Naval Volunteer Reserve, would, most likely, have been part of that preceding roll call had he not died of sepsis in the Greek islands following a mosquito bite. That was on 23 April, ironically the very day originally scheduled for the Cape Helles landings, and 'in sight of the windy plains of Troy', as one soldier would recall it.

It's certainly true that the region's Homeric connection held an extra fascination for a particular class of Englishman such as Brooke, raised with the classics, and evoked typically by, say, Binyon in his poem *Gallipoli*, which begins:

> *Isles of the Aegean, Troy, and waters of Hellespont!*
> *You we have known from of old,*
> *Since boyhood stammering glorious Greek was entranced*
> *In the tale that Homer told.*
> *There scornful Achilles towered and flamed through the battle,*
> *Defying the gods; and there*
> *Hector armed, and Andromache proudly held up his boy to him,*
> *Knowing not yet despair.*

However, Masefield, for his account of the campaign, published in 1916, eschewed Greek myth for an alternative literary muse, the eleventh century epic poem, *The Song of Roland*, recalling Charlemagne's crusade against Saracen Muslims in Spain.

His beautifully-written but surprisingly uncritical account of Gallipoli – that it was 'dedicated with the deepest admiration and respect' to General Hamilton and his officers and men' might be a clue – feels almost like some sort of retro apologia for the campaign.

Whether his clearly ardent sentiments, typified by the following, might have been compensation for individual loss is decidedly moot.

As each ship crammed with soldiers drew near the battleship the men swung their caps and cheered again, and the soldiers answered, and the noise of cheering swelled, and the men in the ships not yet moving joined in, and the men ashore, till all the life in the harbour was giving thanks that it could go to death rejoicing. All was beautiful in that gladness of men about to die, but the most moving thing was the greatness of their generous hearts.

Herbert's *The Secret Battle* and Raymond's *Tell England* (followed thirty-five years later by an unofficial sequel, *The Quiet Shore*), were thinly-disguised autobiographical novels, published shortly after the war, and still redolent with the white heat of first-hand experience. Though, certainly in Raymond's case, overly sentimental, both remain profound testaments to the futility and waste of war.

The latter, a huge bestseller which was re-printed no fewer than twenty times within two years of its publication in 1922, also offered in its final lines, mingling passionately both poignancy and patriotism, an epitaph to the star-crossed campaign, which might also have been referring to George's subsequent sacrifice.

Tell England – You must write a book and tell 'em, Rupert, about the dead schoolboys of your generation – Tell England, ye who pass this monument, we died for her, and here we rest content.

* * *

My principal thanks must be reserved for George T. Drewry, only surviving nephew of my young hero, as well as his cousin, Heather Thorne, daughter of Ronald Kendall. They graciously welcomed my intrusion into their family history and both, separately, provided invaluable research materials, printed, hand-written and photographic.

George's own letters were not only fascinating in their own right but also whetted the appetite for the bigger picture. The extensive extracts I used were, on occasion, subject to (I hope) sensitive amendments to spelling, punctuation and syntax for greater ease of reading.

This book is not intended to be a comprehensive history of the Dardanelles campaign, rather an attempt to reflect a singular portrait through the recollections of one young man, along with an attempt to paint an accurate backcloth against which he and his colleagues fought their war.

It is also, albeit to a lesser extent, the story of a whole family in which George was just one of four siblings who all experienced at first hand the Great War and its terrible consequences on land and at sea.

To this end, and as an enthusiastic rather than a scholarly historian, I am particularly grateful for the support, encouragement and, in certain cases, active assistance of some of Gallipoli's most distinguished contemporary chroniclers including Nigel Steel, Steve Chambers, Peter Hart, Peter Doyle, and Stephen Snelling – the 'usual suspects', some might say – who have helped vividly to fashion the mountain of fine literature already on the subject. Snelling's exhaustively-researched *The Wooden Horse of Gallipoli*, which was published only last year, was particularly helpful. I would echo Steven Spielberg who once wrote, 'we steal from the same people, providing of course they are the best people'.

I have been a biographer for many years, attempting to re-create as accurately as possible the past and present lives of actors, writers, directors and even the occasional murderer. But striving, this time round, to put flesh on the bones of a modest young sailor who died among millions of other, many similarly heroic no doubt, in that war a century ago, required a whole new skillset; not least in the matter of military history, itself a minefield, if you'll pardon the expression, of subjective interpretation.

Guidance was the key. So thanks to Clive Harris, battlefield tour guide extraordinary who first fired me up with passion for the subject, and then to Clive's pal, naval historian Steve Hunnisett, who answered a stream of questions with unfailing patience and good humour before directing me where and when necessary towards relevant sources such as the National Archives, Kew; the British Library; National Maritime Museum, Greenwich; the Maritime History Archive, Newfoundland; and, of course, the Imperial War Museum, which first forged a link with the Drewry family just months after George's death.

Without the aid of my friend and former cricketing colleague, Commodore Mike Bath RN, I would never have benefited from the help and resources of The Office of the Naval Secretary, Navy Command HQ or Stephen Prince, Deputy Head of the Naval Staff (Strategic Analysis & Records) and Head of Naval Historical Branch/ Head of Specialism for Historians in the Ministry of Defence.

A number of the photographs in this book are from the family collections and, where requested, credit has been given to other sources. Where an appropriate acknowledgment has proved impossible owing to lack of information, this will be rectified in any future printings.

Helping to fill in various gaps in the Drewry family history were: Skye Holland, George's great niece; Sally Gilbert, archivist, Merchant Taylors' School, Northwood; Debbie Beckett, Central Library, Grimsby; Phil Melladay, Lincoln Inspire Ltd; Reverend Canon Jeremy Fraser, Nanette Johnson-Reid, Delores Small, All Saints Church, Forest Gate; David Mackie, Orkney Library and Archive; Angus Konstam, Orkney and military historian; Beth Ellis, Curator, Digital Collections and Web Editor, P&O Heritage Collection; Heritage Archives, Stratford Library; The City of London Corporation; Nigel Gardiner, Drewry Shipping Consultants; David Hughes, Royal Yacht

Squadron; Sheila Newsome, Selby and District Family History Group; Yusuf Kaayalp and Baris Yesildag at Canakkale, and DC Thomson Ltd.

Also to Herbie Kretzmer for introducing me to *The Great War and Modern Memory*; Michael J. Whelan for permission to quote from his poem 'Gallipoli' (2012); Roger Moston; Michael Tedham; John Mackenzie, who re-visited Gallipoli with me in 2017, somehow managed to get injured above V Beach, and contributed my maps; Richard Tedham, whose tireless research assistance was often above and beyond; the production staff at Pen & Sword, whose commissioning editor, Brigadier Henry Wilson, encouraged me from the outset; my editor Irene Moore whose suggestions were always constructive and helpful; finally, my wife Anthea whose pursuit of her own family history drew me to Gallipoli in the first place.

Little Marlow / Canakkale / Scapa Flow
2017 / 2018

Chapter 1

V Beach, 25 April (am)

A good army of 50,000 men and sea power – that is the end of the Turkish menace.

Winston Churchill

You are just simply eaten up with the Dardanelles and cannot think of anything else! Damn the Dardanelles! They will be our grave!

Admiral Jacky Fisher to Churchill

If it had been scripted by Hollywood then the story of George Drewry and his heroic Great War exploits, which figure at the very heart of a short, accident-prone, life might have started something like this.

> *'I have been ordered to report for active service, sir,' said George Drewry, as he stepped into his commander's cabin on the P&O liner at Port Said.*
>
> *'Well, goodbye my boy,' said the commander gripping the young officer's hand warmly: 'you will keep the old flag flying?' He was sorry to part with the modest lad who was so competent for his 18 years.*
>
> *'I will do my best, sir,' said young Drewry.*

This suitably stiff-upper-lip if entirely fanciful dialogue, which also manages rather sloppily to reduce George's age by a year, actually arrived courtesy of an article from a popular series called, promisingly, *Stories From Real Life* which appeared regularly in a now defunct Australian morning daily newspaper, the *Melbourne Argus*.

Intriguingly, the account, which is reprinted in full towards the end of this book, is not remotely contemporaneous but was in fact published in 1937, more than two decades on from the ill-fated Anglo–French invasion of the Gallipoli peninsula which began on 25 April 1915, just a couple of days after the Germans first unleashed poisonous gas on the Western Front at the Second Battle of Ypres.

The grand plan for 25 April was hatched after an earlier Allied naval attempt to force the Dardanelles, fatally undermine the Ottoman Empire and open the road to Constantinople, had failed dismally.

For George, the day that would change his life began shortly after 2am that Sunday when, sleepily, he relieved his captain, Commander Edward Unwin, on the bridge of the *River Clyde*, a requisitioned old collier that would become known as 'The Wooden Horse of Gallipoli'.

George wrote nearly three weeks later to his father: 'I found myself with only the helmsman, steering towards the Turkish searchlights on a calm night just making headway against the current, shadowy forms of destroyers and battleships slipping past me. Visions of mines and submarines rose before me as I thought of the 2½ thousand *[sic]* men in the holds and I felt very young.'

An hour or so later, Unwin returned to the bridge giving George the opportunity to try and grab some more sleep. Barely, as it transpired, because he soon received an urgent message from the captain to take charge of the steam hopper *Argyle*, a flat-bottomed barge, which was attached to lighters at the side of the ship.

It was an 'anxious time', continued George, with typical understatement, as 'we steered towards Cape Helles'. Within minutes of casting off from the *River Clyde* with his crew of six Greek sailors and seaman 'Geordie' Samson, Allied ships began a furious bombardment of the Turkish shoreline. It was now shortly after 5am …

George had been stationed at Mudros with his own ship, HMS *Hussar*, for over a month before he made his first close acquaintance of the *River Clyde* around mid–April.

The port of Mudros, a natural harbour, was set in a large bay about midway along the south side of the Aegean island of Lemnos. A little over 40 nautical miles from Cape Helles, Mudros, throughout March and April, provided an extraordinary spectacle for the soldiers and sailors gathering there for the 'Dardanelles adventure', as described by Captain L.B. Weldon MC in his 1923 memoir, *Hard Lying*.

> 'The great land-locked bay was packed with battleships, transports and colliers. On the island itself camps of British and colonial troops were springing up everywhere and although, as I soon found out, no one seemed to know exactly what was toward, everybody knew that such concentration was not meaningless. The "holiday" could not last for long, and officers and men were all trying their hardest to make the best of it.'

Colliers, in particular, were very much on the mind of *Hussar*'s captain, Commander Unwin, who, towards the end of a joint meeting of the staffs on board the headquarters ship, HMS *Arcadian*, spelled out a novel way, as he recalled later, of landing a huge body of men 'in a specially prepared ship, right on the beach'; in this case, V Beach, one of five beaches – also S, W, X and Y – around Cape Helles, at the western tip of the Gallipoli peninsula, designated as the focal point for the attack.

According to Stephen Snelling: 'Though hardly fully formed, he [Unwin] reasoned that his scheme meant that "the troops would be safe from rifle fire till they tried to leave the ship". He realised the plan was not without hazard. His greatest fear and only danger that he could foresee was from heavy guns sited on the shore, but, as he understood it, such a threat was not anticipated.'

It seems the general reaction around the table was initially unfavourable – typically, too many eggs in one vulnerable basket. Until, that is, the arrival at the meeting, after Unwin left, of Rear Admiral Rosslyn Erskine 'Rosy' Wemyss, who, as Governor of Lemnos, was charged with preparing the harbour for the Dardanelles operation. With his support, which was then formalised swiftly at the highest level, Unwin got the go-ahead to 'take any ship I liked in the harbour and fit her out as I liked to carry out my scheme'.

As well as a conduit for landing men, the ship should also, Unwin suggested, carry 700 tons of fresh water for immediate use and be able to condense a further 100 tons a day. After the actual landing, it would then serve as a stores depot and as a shelter where wounded could receive treatment before despatch to hospital ships.

Unwin's eye fell very quickly on the Glasgow-built *River Clyde*, just under 4,000 tonnes and some 345ft in length, which had plied the world's shipping lanes for some ten years before fetching up in Mudros under charter to the French military. Within twenty-four hours Unwin had secured, not without some Gallic opposition, its immediate release and ordered her to go alongside the naval repair ship, HMS *Reliance*, 'to have her fitted out for her novel work'.

Meanwhile George, who had recently been joined by two more midshipmen on *Hussar*, was, as the great armada around him readied for action, beginning to tire of doing nothing after endless days in harbour apart from sharing close watches with his fellow junior officers.

> 'So I asked the Captain for more work; well, I got it with a vengeance. He took me on board this ship and gave me thirty Greeks and told me to clean her. Well, she was the dirtiest ship I've seen. She was in ballast and had just brought French mules up from Algiers, they had built boxes and floors in the tween decks and carried the mules there without worrying about sanitary arrangements.'

Intriguingly, presumably for censorship purposes, the name *River Clyde* is never mentioned once in the letter and George's first choice of 'filthiest' is crossed out in favour of 'dirtiest'.

Despite his considerable youth, George was chosen by Unwin to be his second-in-command on the converted collier, helping to lead a select group of officers and men from *Hussar* – volunteers all – who also included the warrant engineer, William Horend, the ship's carpenter, Irish surgeon Peter Burrowes Kelly and experienced seamen such as Samson and William Williams.

Unwin had, he revealed in a long letter to Wemyss (later Lord Wester-Wemyss) some years after the war, asked the existing crew of *River Clyde* if they wished to volunteer for the enterprise but recalled the Master, John Kerr, telling him, 'we will do all we can to help you prepare the ship but I don't think you can expect us to be there when the bricks begin to fly about'. In fact there was to be one addition to the ship's new company; none other than Kerr's 37-year-old younger brother, Charles, the original steward, Glasgow-born like his vessel, 'apparently having more guts than his brother', noted Unwin, a little acidly.

The eventual crew – twenty-four in total – was tiny compared with the enormous human cargo that would shortly be assigned to the innards of the ship; principally, 2,000 troops mainly from the 1st Battalion Royal Dublin and 1st Battalion Royal Munster Fusiliers along with sappers from the 1st (West Riding) Field Company and two companies of the 2nd Hampshires.

To provide covering fire from on board, a unit of the Royal Naval Armoured Car Squadron, led by Lieutenant Commander (later Lord) Josiah Wedgwood, great-great grandson of the Staffordshire potter and an MP since 1906, also joined the ship's strength. Other support units included men of the 89th (1st Highland) Field Ambulance, Royal Army Medical Corps, and a platoon from the Royal Naval Division's Anson Battalion, which included the 24-year-old scholar and poet, Sub Lieutenant Arthur 'Pog' Tisdall, to supply beach parties.

In addition, there were a pair of lieutenant colonels, Charles 'Dick' Doughty-Wylie, a Sudan, Boer War and Boxer Rebellion veteran, and Weir de Lancey Williams, later a major general, acting as liaison officers for Sir Ian Hamilton, the commander-in-chief. They 'had wriggled on board, I never discovered quite why, but there they were,' recorded Unwin.

Last but not least, a pair of donkeys were ushered aboard.

To the crew and the troops, Unwin and George must have appeared a strikingly contrasting pair at the helm of this unique undertaking.

As described by Australian historian Les Carlyon, Unwin 'had escaped from an unwritten novel by Joseph Conrad. He was more than six feet tall, strongly made, with a small thin mouth and a jutting chin. He bawled out orders through a megaphone and didn't spare the stragglers or the dim-witted … he had earned the right to roar out orders and he was well-liked; colleagues described him as cheerful and good humoured.'

'Huge and bluff', the *News of the World* would later portray Unwin, who had first been commissioned into the Royal Navy as a lieutenant from the Mercantile Marine, as the Merchant Navy was then known, in 1895 at the age of 31. During his career he had become an expert on the fast coaling of ships. Although retired, on the eve of war, he was recalled to the service and appointed to the Staff of Admiral Sir John Jellicoe as Fleet Coaling Officer at Scapa Flow. He took command of *Hussar* two months before the landings.

Experienced as he was, there's clearly no doubt that his ambitious plan still weighed very heavy on the grizzled, hawk-nosed, 51-year-old, as he would confess to Wemyss:

> 'I have never spent such a time in my life as I did before the landing, the awful responsibility, for I wasn't just carrying out orders, but varying through a scheme of my own in which, if I failed, the consequences might be awful. The thousands of thoughts that flash through one's head at such a time as to what might happen and how to meet them. And on top of it all the wonder as to how one will behave oneself, as I don't believe any man is quite sure of himself.'

More than thirty years Unwin's junior, who shared with his captain previous service for the steamship company P&O, George, at 20, was described by Surgeon Kelly as being of 'medium height but powerfully built … very good looking, modest and charming'.

In a brief but extremely colourful pamphlet titled *With Machine Guns in Gallipoli*, published in 1915, Lieutenant Commander Wedgwood characterized the two officers with something of a literary flourish, as 'a dug-out half-pay captain who dreamed of lighters' and 'a midshipman of Adonis-like beauty from the merchant marine'.

Such first-hand descriptions of the younger man remain frustratingly rare so one searches for further clues in some photographs of George across his abbreviated life. They range, among others, from a seven-year-old in 1901 dressed, presciently, in a sailor's tunic, to a 23-year-old, with his lieutenant's stripes, looking mature and somewhat care-worn beyond his years in a shot taken just two days before his death. In between, we find, variously, a handsome 14-year-old, a serious-looking recipient of the VC, and a naval officer in civvies gleefully playing the fool on shore leave.

To accommodate this eclectic throng, *River Clyde* clearly needed much more than just a deep clean; for George and his workforce, it was now a question of adapting the vessel for practical use in the imminent invasion, specifically for disembarking troops as easily, safely and quickly as possible. This required eight ports to be cut in her, four each side, large enough to allow a fully-equipped soldier to pass through to a temporary gallery rigged around the ship leading to the bows. The idea was then that the men would reach shore over a hopper acting as a bridge. But as no one yet quite knew how quickly the beach dropped away, three wooden lighters were also required to fill any possible gap in this *ad hoc* pontoon.

And then, wrote George, 'a party of the armoured car people came on board and rigged small huts of [boiler] plates and sandbags and put Maxims in them.' There were twelve guns in all. Finally, George supervised the painting of the ship's starboard side in the colours of P&O, presumably as an affectionate 'nod' to his and his captain's old firm.

The transformation was all but complete by 19 April, a week after Unwin had first picked out the collier, and just four days away from 23 April – St George's Day – the date originally chosen for the invasion.

However, despite all the preparation, and the *River Clyde* was just one small part of it, they had reckoned without the one thing over which no-one could have control – the weather, which had, crucially, to be settled for such an expedition involving the landing of scores of small craft around a headland where currents are fierce.

As Brigadier General Aspinall-Oglander would record later in his official history of the campaign:

> 'At that moment so far as the elements were concerned, the prospect was alarming. The glass spoke only of danger; the wind was blowing hard, with driving showers from the north-east. Throughout the whole preparatory period the caprice of the weather had been a source of unending trouble and anxiety.'

So the landing had to be postponed, first for twenty-four hours, then for forty-eight. Thankfully, however, the morning of 23 April dawned fine, and Admiral John de Robeck, who commanded the Allied naval forces, ordered the movement of some 200 ships finally to begin.

Some time between noon and 1pm, the *River Clyde* went to sea, towing three lighters and, on its port side, a steamboat, with the steam hopper, *Argyle*, on the starboard. As soon as they were clear of the main shipping, the lighters were dropped astern.

'Can you imagine how proud I felt,' George told his father, 'as we steamed down the line, I on the fo'castle head. The flagship wished us luck as we passed. As soon as the tow was dropped I took the bridge until the Captain had had lunch, then I had mine and carried on with the work, for there were many things to be done.'

First port of call was the island of Tenedos, 35 nautical miles to the east of Mudros, which would be the final jumping-off point on 25 April for all the ships allotted to the Cape Helles landings. The *River*

Clyde steamed into Tenedos just before the sun set and anchored, although George's working day didn't finish until midnight – with a brief interruption for a pheasant dinner, courtesy of the captain of the *Soudan*, a P&O vessel turned hospital ship.

The calm sea of that day was replaced next morning by something rather different. 'It was blowing fresh at daylight,' recalled Unwin, quite mildly. 'Things looked bad,' George suggested instead, 'a nasty breeze made us afraid the show would not come off, but it died quickly.' At around 10am a signal was passed to the *River Clyde*, 'telling us we were in someone's berth, and for an hour we wandered among the ships with our long tail just scraping along ships' sides and across their bows. We were nobody's dog, nobody loved us.'

As the *River Clyde*, with all its accessory craft was, it seems, unable to have its foremost stages fully rigged with the anchor down, Unwin urgently needed to tie up to another ship to complete this crucial work. After steaming bulkily around the crowded harbour, he finally found 'our old friend' *Fauvette*, an armed boarding steamer, to which she could secure on the eve of the invasion for the finishing touches.

From around 4pm a stream of fleet sweepers packed with troops began to come alongside the *River Clyde*; 'in capital spirits,' noted Unwin, 'and stowed themselves away for the night'.

Stephen Snelling: 'They came burdened with gear that included 200 rounds of ammunition, a full pack and haversack, a waterproof sheet, some firewood, three days' iron rations which might have to last five days and a full water bottle, which was not to be drunk from without permission as it was thought possible the Turks had poisoned the wells on the peninsula. All told, every man carried 80lb of kit, all of which had to be crammed into the cramped holds.'

No wonder the expression, 'Black hole of Calcutta' soon became common currency among the packed soldiery.

Before George was sent off at 11.30pm to try and snatch some sleep, Unwin held a dinner party 'in my so-called ward room of all my crowd plus as many of the regimental officers as we could seat, for many of whom,' he recorded, sadly, 'it was their last dinner.'

The *River Clyde* sailed at midnight, beginning the 14-mile crossing to Cape Helles. 'It was a perfectly calm night,' Unwin wrote, 'and we could see the Chanak search light the whole way and most useful it proved to me as owing to the amount of iron I had put round the bridge, my compass hadn't much idea where the North Pole was.' Chanak was the enemy town of Canakkale opposite the peninsula.

Before us lies an adventure unprecedented in modern war. Together with our comrades of the fleet we are about to force a landing upon an open beach in face of positions which have been vaunted by our enemies as impregnable. The landing will be made good by the help of God and the navy; the positions will be stormed, and the war brought one step nearer to a glorious close.

Sir Ian Hamilton

Chapter 2

North and South

What machines we are on board of a man-of-war!
We walk, talk, eat, drink, sleep, and get up,
just like clockwork; we are wound up to go
the twenty four hours, and then wound up again.

Mr Midshipman Easy

George's nautical future might have been predestined from the moment his father Thomas Drewry shook off the legacy of several lifetimes to become a marine engineer. Born in 1859, Thomas was descended from generations of North East Lincolnshire blacksmiths – including his father, John Drewry, a native of Cleethorpes, then a budding seaside resort just a stone's throw from the mouth of the River Humber.

In the mid to late nineteenth century, Lincolnshire, stretching from the Humber in the north to Cambridgeshire in the south, was a county best known for its plenteous agriculture and burgeoning fishing industry, the latter centring on Grimsby, three miles from the Drewry family home.

Two years before Thomas, the youngest of seven children, was born, there were just twenty-two vessels in the North Sea port; by the time he was four that number had escalated to 112. At the turn of the century, there were no fewer than a thousand fishing trawlers at Grimsby. Clearly there was no better time for a marine-based future in that neck of the woods, and Thomas served his apprenticeship with the Manchester, Sheffield and Lincolnshire Railway Company at its Grimsby Docks fitting shop. The MS&LR, which in 1897 would change its name to the Great Central Railway ahead of opening its

London extension, operated a number of ships from mid-nineteenth century onwards, starting with the SS *Albert* which was launched in 1856.

In 1882 Thomas ventured south for the first time when he joined the Peninsular and Oriental Steam Navigation Company (P&O) as an engineer at Tilbury Docks. By then P&O had already been in operation for half a century, principally building its reputation as a reliable mail carrying service, initially to the Iberian Peninsula and thereafter points east, most notably in 1854, taking over the lucrative Bombay mail service from the mighty East India Company.

A couple of years on, Thomas returned north to marry Mary Ann, a year his junior and first of ten children to George and Naomi Kendall of Great Grimsby. Naomi was also born a Drewry, the daughter of a blacksmith, also called George, a native, too, of north-east Lincolnshire. A careful study of the family tree reveals that George and John were actually brothers, born two years apart to Matthew and Pleasant Drewry, so Thomas and Mary Ann were, in fact, cousins.

Their wedding took place at Holy Trinity and St Mary the Virgin, Old Clee – said to be the oldest building in Grimsby dating from Saxon times – twenty-five years after Thomas was baptized there. The church was less than two miles from the Kendall family home at Intax Farm, off Welholme Road, which comprised a cottage and some ten acres of land. 'Intax' is unusual; it took its name from 'intake', which described the actions of the abbot when he enclosed part of the lands of the Lordship of Weelsby – once a settlement in its own right to the east of Grimsby – with a ring fence.

Thomas's oldest brother, incidentally, was named Drewry, known as 'Drew', and the intermingling of Christian names would continue in the extended family down the generations.

Thomas and Mary Ann's first child, Harry Kendall, was born in 1888 at Intax Farm which suggests Mary Ann had returned to her parents' home for the birth despite the fact she and Thomas were, by now, permanently resident in East London because of his job with

P&O. In fact, it's likely that Thomas had swapped Tilbury for the Royal Albert Docks where he would remain for the rest of his career with the company, rising eventually to assistant superintendent and manager of P&O's ship repairing operation at the site.

When their second son, Herbert Percy – known as Percy – arrived in 1890, there's some confusion as to quite where he was actually born. His birth certificate records him living in Glenparke Road, Forest Gate, but there is a handwritten entry in one of the family archives which notes he was born in Bombay, where his father was posted for two years towards the end of the 1880s. It may be that Mary Ann, who, one presumes, was with her husband, had travelled home from India to give birth to Percy.

What is certain is that from now on the Drewrys were firmly established in Forest Gate. The little terraced house in Glenparke Road and then another in Haslemere Road, both south of the busy east/west Romford Road, were succeeded by a pair of considerably smarter homes to the north of that main thoroughfare, starting with 15 Hampton Road and finally, 58 Claremont Road, both substantial detached properties with, as the census would note, 'a servant'. It was almost as if they had proverbially crossed the tracks.

When George Leslie and Ralph were born in 1894 and 1898, respectively, completing the quartet of sons, the family still lived at Haslemere Road, but by the time they moved to Hampton Road their former address had – ironically in view of his major part in the catastrophe which would eventually engulf the family – changed its name to Kitchener Road, doubtless to laud the so-called achievements of Lord Kitchener in the recently resolved Boer Wars. It was interesting also to note that the Drewrys gave number 58 a new house name, 'Welholme', so quite literally, linking the family's north/south connection.

By the time the Drewrys made their permanent home in Forest Gate – today part of the rampantly multi-cultural inner London borough of Newham where mosques, temples and Sikh Gurdwara now outnumber churches – it had evolved during Victorian times from a small clump of houses round a barrier to Epping Forest into, as a local online history put it, 'that area to the south of Wanstead Flats' which became 'recognizably a London suburb' whose 'streets and villas ... were an oasis of middle class, suburban, tranquillity'.

Key to the pace of the development was the forging of good transport links. The Eastern Counties Railway had opened its London to Romford Line in 1839 and a station was built at Forest Gate. The London Tilbury and Southend Railway opened its line, which ran through Forest Gate, in 1858, and by the turn of the century some 350,000 passengers a month were using the station. Tramways opened along the Romford Road in 1886 and yet another railway, the Tottenham & Forest Gate line, made its bow in 1894 providing connections into Moorgate and St Pancras, ideal for city workers.

Once the family had moved above Romford Road, it was only a short walk north to the aforementioned Flats, the most southern part of Epping Forest, a spectacular open grassland of some 334 acres with its bandstand (now gone), ponds, football pitches and popular Bank Holiday fairs. It was also big enough, later, to be the site of prisoner-of-war camps during the Second World War and for defensive artillery.

For Thomas Drewry, Forest Gate perfectly suited his commutes, first to Tilbury and then the Royal Albert Docks, the latter only about three miles as the crow flies. The dock, with its three miles of quay and convenient entrance to the Thames, opened in 1880. The area is recognizable today because London City Airport's single runway was constructed right along the south side of the dock itself, 130 years after it was a hub of trade and industry. Now it is in the early stages of a huge, Chinese-led, regeneration project, due to be completed in 2026.

Thomas's rising status with P&O would be enough eventually to help prompt the entry of all four sons into employment with the same company. But first came their education. Harry, according to his Naval service record, attended the Carpenters' Company Institute in Jupp Road, Stratford – which had become a day school in 1891, then West

Ham Technical Institute. It's likely that Percy followed in his footsteps before both older Drewry boys became apprenticed to P&O.

George may well have been a Carpenters' Company pupil, too, to begin with, but as far as his recorded education is concerned, the newspapers, in the wake of his subsequent VC deeds, would, almost to a man, solely credit 'Merchant Taylors, Blackheath', as his youthful seat of learning. Quite how this came to be perpetuated down the years remains a mystery as the venerable public school's official history would reveal that Blackheath doesn't figure at all in Merchant Taylors' chronology or geography.

MTS had, since its founding in 1561, always been firmly a City of London-bound establishment, first at Suffolk Lane, between Upper Thames Street and Cannon Street, before switching, a little over three centuries later, to the Charterhouse, just off Aldersgate, after that eponymous public school made its own final move way out of town to Godalming in Surrey.

Quite why George, unlike Harry and Percy, got the opportunity of a private education remains unexplained except to suggest that as, by the early 1900s, Thomas was in a senior position with P&O, he could now afford to splash out on at least one of his offspring. The family had already suffered a blow when Ralph, aged four or five, was struck down with scarlet fever which resulted in severe hearing loss, so his future education was inevitably fated to be carefully specialized.

Shortly after the turn of the century, MTS appointed its twenty-third headmaster, John Arbuthnot Nairn, an Irishman from Dublin who, unlike fifteen of his predecessors, was not an old boy of the school. By the time George, on the cusp of 13, made his debut at the Charterhouse in 1907, benefiting in no small way from those improved rail connections out of Forest Gate and into the city, Nairn's reign was firmly established. Certainly, as F.W.M. Draper's *Four Centuries of Merchant Taylors' School* proclaims, 'no greater scholar had ever been headmaster of the school'. He was however, Draper also notes, 'without an assistant master's experience of schools' and MTS was beginning to suffer, in terms of school numbers, from the rise of other good and less expensive schools in and around London.

Indeed it was Nairn who first began to ponder the audacious idea of moving the school to the outskirts of the capital, which eventually transpired in 1933, six years after he ceased to be head.

Browsing through a faded but still elegant, blue and gold leather-tooled volume, 'Merchant Taylors' School Probation List, 1907 to 1913', mentions of George are few and far between. He's there a little below halfway in the Form Order for Upper First Form, a class of twenty-nine, in which he's the second oldest, while the youngest, five places above him, is barely 10. A year on, in Lower Second, he has climbed to tenth out of thirty-four. There's an early commendation for his French followed later by below average marks for the same subject as well as in Mathematics.

Soon after he arrived at the school, George would probably have witnessed the unveiling of a memorial to one of MTS's most distinguished old boys, Robert Clive (of India) by Lord George Curzon, a former Viceroy of India who had been recently elected Chancellor of Oxford University. Clive was just one of many OMTs (Old Merchant Taylors) along with poets like Edmund Spenser and Robert Herrick, the painter Samuel Palmer, dramatist John Webster, surgeon Sir Frederick Treves, clerics such as the Most Reverend William Juxon and Lancelot Andrewes, Bishop of Winchester, and even the odd actor like Boris Karloff (when he was still plain William Henry Pratt).

While there's no record of his involvement in any games, at which MTS particularly excelled, it's likely that George may well have taken an interest in the cadet corps which, in 1908, along with similar outfits in other English schools was organized into a single body called the Officers' Training Corps or OTC. It's often said that the officering of the new armies in 1914 would have been even more difficult than it was without the establishment of the OTC.

Less than two years after arriving at the school, George had become, at 14, one of the younger OMTs as he prepared for a new life in the Mercantile Marine. It would be another eight years before he'd make a triumphant return to the school, in November 1916 at the age of 22, a year after being widely acclaimed a national hero.

With his disability, Ralph's education was, naturally, much more problematical. He first attended Water Lane Board school, a stiff walk west down the Romford Road. The school first opened in 1897 for 1,478 pupils on a large site, which also included a deaf and dumb centre, a pupil-teacher centre and school board officers.

Before George left home in 1909 on an almost permanent basis, he and Ralph were, according to his younger brother, very close. Years later he told writer Michael Moynihan:

'George was wonderful to me. We were always together as boys, like twins. I often think of those days. My earliest memory is when we were small children playing in Wanstead Park and we stepped into a bog. We sank and sank, right up to our necks, until a passer-by heard our cries and hauled us out. I remember my father gave the man a new suit. I suppose if it hadn't been for him we would have drowned.'

This was the first recorded example of the 'accident-prone' tag, which would pursue George throughout his life. It was followed a few years later when he was 13 with another potentially fatal mishap. While on holiday visiting his maternal grandparents at Intax Farm, he was knocked down and unconscious by a car in Welholme Road. Happily, there were no long-lasting effects except, perhaps, a heightened survival instinct.

After George went to sea, Ralph was sent away to boarding school, special in more senses than one. The Mount, at Penkhull, near Stoke-on-Trent, was built in 1803 as a family home by celebrated china manufacturer, Josiah Spode II. After Spodes various died or moved away during the century, the house eventually was taken over by the North Staffordshire Blind and Deaf School in 1897, under the inspirational leadership of its first headmaster, Arthur J. Story, who later became Secretary of the National Institute for the Deaf in London.

The UK Census for 1911 recorded Percy as being the only one of the three Drewry sons still living at home in Claremont Road, along with his parents and two servants. Three years later, he was the furthest from home, in Kobe, Japan, apparently the youngest-ever P&O employee to be sent to foreign climes, when, on 28 June 1914, at Sarajevo, a shot rang out 'that was heard round the world'.

> *Fair broke the day this morning*
> *Against the Dardanelles;*
> *The breeze blew soft, the morn's cheeks*
> *Were cold as cold sea-shells.*
>
> *But other shells are waiting*
> *Across the Aegean sea,*
> *Shrapnel and high explosive,*
> *Shells and hells for me.*

Patrick Shaw-Stewart

Chapter 3

On the Ocean Wave

Commanding the pinnace was a midshipman of His Majesty's Navy, a 'snotty'. I really think these boys – you can call them nothing else – are the bravest of all Britain's brave. Certainly they are second to none. Among all the branches of our services that I have worked with, I have never seen quite their match. Yet for the most part they are downy-faced lads, soft-skinned, warm from home and mothering.

Major A.H. Mure TD

If, as the rousing patriotic anthem still continues to insist 'Britannia Rules the Waves', then the historic bedrock of this obstinately-unshakeable oceangoing imperialism must surely be the midshipman, lowest form but, undeniably, hardest-working of the commissioned naval officer class.

According to Dr Samantha Cavell, author of a *Social History of Midshipmen*:

'The origin of the midshipman's rating is obscure, with some reports of "midschipmen" dating back as far as the mid-fourteenth century. The application of the term in a modern sense, for a "working petty officer in big ships", was in use by the 1630s, and throughout the 1660s and 1670s the rating of "midshipman" was generally filled by an experienced seaman – someone who might aspire to a warrant officer's rating, but not to commissioned rank.'

With the introduction in 1676 by Samuel Pepys of a new volunteer-per order system for the Royal Navy, and the need to qualify these midshipmen as seaman on their way to commissioned rank, the meaning of the rating diversified so that several different types of midshipmen could be active aboard any given ship.

First was 'the well-born young gentleman who, having completed his two years as a volunteer per order, was engaged in his third year of training as a midshipman.'

Second was 'the captain's (or officer's) servant who, having entered under the patronage of a commissioned officer, had completed his two years of basic seamanship in the rating of servant, or another entry-level rating.'

The third represented 'those who rose from the lower deck on merit alone and whose highest aspiration was that of warrant officer.'

Fourth was 'the midshipman ordinary. This classification referred to a former volunteer per order or volunteer of the Royal Naval Academy, borne as a midshipman additional to complement. A midshipman ordinary took the place and pay of an able seaman, but was otherwise rated as a supernumerary midshipman.'

Fifth was designated 'midshipman extraordinary, to provide employment for ex-commanders or lieutenants, by carrying them over and above the ordinary complement established for the ship in which they sailed.'

Initially called 'reformadoes', the position of 'midshipman extraordinary' was available only to officers whose records were clear of 'any misdemeanour or failure of duty in their previous command'. Only a limited number of openings for midshipmen extraordinary were ever available and made for serious competition among unemployed officers.

From the turn of the century on, those various ratings slowly died out one by one so that by the Napoleonic era, a period especially beloved by best-selling authors of nautical fiction – such as C.S. Forester, Patrick O'Brian, Alexander Kent and, of course, Captain Marryat – the midshipman was generally an apprentice officer who had previously served at least three years as a volunteer, officer's servant or able seaman, and was roughly equivalent to a present-day petty officer in rank and responsibilities.

While the fully decentralized system of recruitment, which existed up until 1815, allowed the possibility of greater social diversity among the corps of officer aspirants, 'selection and appointment decisions,' noted Dr Cavell, 'remained susceptible to the demands of the social elites. Recruiting captains were, however, answerable only to their personal and professional interests, which could vary with the state of war, the demands of the service, and their own financial, social, or political ambitions.

'What changed after 1815 was that these variables were slowly eliminated allowing the will of the Admiralty to be carried out more effectively. A by-product of these changes was the increasingly limited opportunity for social mobility among officer aspirants.

'In the years after Napoleon's defeat only those with pedigree and powerful interest had a real shot at career success. It was a structure that would crystallize in the decades to come and one which defined the Royal Navy's officer corps well into the twentieth century,' Dr Cavell concluded.

Not that, historically, life afloat was any easier for the genteel. Ben Wilson, in his *Empire of the Deep: The Rise and Fall of the British Navy*, writes: 'Accident of birth was crucial. But there was an added factor in the late eighteenth century. This was an age when more was expected of commissioned officers. It was no longer good enough to be an accomplished seaman and/or well-connected. The sons of gentlemen sent to sea at a tender age were treated as ratings, sent aloft to work with the topmen and to do menial tasks. They had to learn to splice, reef and knot.'

'Middies' or 'snotties', as they were often termed supposedly due to the young gentlemen's habit of wiping their noses with their sleeves, also had to learn mathematics, astronomy and navigation – not to mention everything from languages to dancing for possible advancement – and, adds Wilson, 'as part of their training were required to sketch coastlines and map shoals to help provide the Admiralty with a database of topographical information.

Despite his commission, a midshipman was not necessarily immune from the indignities regularly heaped on an ordinary seaman. In 1797 the Royal Navy's bloodiest-ever mutiny took place on board HMS *Hermione*, partly triggered by the flogging meted out to Midshipman David Casey who had dared to remonstrate with his sadistic captain over the use of abusive language.

Such extremes of senior officer behaviour and the varied reactions of underlings, all set against a backcloth of seagoing peril, naturally fuelled and colourfully flavoured the ripping fictional yarns of midshipman characters, without exception comparatively well-born, like Forester's Horatio Hornblower, Kent's Richard Bolitho, O'Brian's William Babbington (re-named, and much elevated to, Lord Blakeney in the 2003 film version) and Marryat's Jack Easy.

> *A midshipman was neither fish nor fowl. He stood between the lieutenants and the backbone of the vessel, the warrant officers. At one end of the ship, aloof and unreachable like some sort of god, was the captain. Above, around and beyond the overcrowded midshipmen's berth were the ship's company.*
>
> Alexander Kent, *Midshipman Bolitho*

This, according to naval literature aficionado, Colin Fleming, 'is the catch with the best midshipman literature: that 17-year-old, pressed into his own kind of unique service, is both of his age and station and, in a sense, of our age and station, no matter where we may be as adults.

'The notion of being something redoubtable, and still needing to progress, is perhaps the ultimate catch, too, of adulthood, the rock on which so many people founder. So now we have a literature of youth, in part meant as a means in which to chart a course through later years. A different make of ship's model.'

'How can you expect any piece of machinery to go well, so damnably knocked about as a midshipman is', replied our hero.

Mr Midshipman Easy

Although, like his fictional counterparts, heroic to a fault, George's naval path, cleaved from rather humbler roots, seems happily to belie the generalised thrust of Dr Cavell's careful research. An exception to the rule?

That might certainly seem to be the case when contrasted, for instance, with two other midshipmen, both much younger than George, who not only served at Gallipoli but also had their own revealing accounts of youthful service at the Dardanelles published.

Although a slim volume, *From Dartmouth to the Dardanelles*, by the splendidly-named, and decidedly patrician, son of an Hon., Wolstan Beaumont Charles Weld Forester, is a very readable narrative constructed from memory during a spell of sick leave in December 1915.

After the regulation two years at Osborne College on the Isle of Wight followed by just one term at Dartmouth, beginning 7 May 1914, Weld Forester went to war still some weeks shy of his fifteenth birthday. His account ends with the sinking of his ship, HMS *Goliath* – never actually named in the book due to censorship – at the hands of an Ottoman battleship in Morto Bay on 13 May 1915. He was one of less than 200 to survive from a crew of 750.

Even more fascinating than his own jottings are, arguably, the thoughts of his mother Elispeth, which bookend the text. It was her idea to publish (in June 1916) and she who also carefully edited her son's words. In London to meet her son on his return from the sea in June 1915, she writes movingly, echoing what must have been the reaction of so many desperate parents:

'I had not seen him since he left for Dartmouth, nearly fourteen months before. Then he was a round-faced, rosy boy ... Up the step, dragging a seaman's canvas kit-bag, came a tall, thin, figure, white of face, drawn, haggard – incredibly old. I had not quite realised this. For a second my heart stood still – where was my boy? Then he saw me waiting in the hall, and his face lighted up with half-incredulous joyous wonder: "Mother! You here!" My boy was gone for ever – but my son had come home.'

Weld Forester rose to lieutenant commander in the Royal Navy before joining the Diplomatic Service as, first, a vice-consul, then consul and finally consul-general for nearly thirty years in locations ranging from Tangier and Munich to Basra and Nice. He died in 1961, aged 62.

H.M. 'Henry Mangles' Denham's memoir, *Dardanelles: A Midshipman's Diary*, didn't appear until 1981, by which time he was already the acclaimed writer of a series of Mediterranean Sea Guides and a pillar of the Royal Yacht Squadron. The direct descendant of an eponymous vice admiral who was not only knighted for his services to hydrography but also had a town in Western Australia and a tree in British Columbia named after him, Denham, later captain, was an unsung hero of at least two more wars and, as with his distinguished forebear, awarded a CMG. He died in 1993 aged 96.

Like Weld Forester, a graduate of Osborne, Denham was in his last term at Dartmouth when, a day after war was declared, the 16-year-old joined the battleship HMS *Agamemnon* at Devonport which, within weeks, began steaming towards an unknown destination.

At Gallipoli midshipmen were prohibited, for security reasons, from keeping journals. Denham defied this by keeping an invaluable private diary which, with rigorous detail, records people, places, ships and action in the theatre of war, from bombardment of the outer forts towards the end of February 1915, through the attack on the Narrows and the landings of April and August, to the final evacuation of the peninsula in January 1916.

A couple of months before Denham and George would share the trials and tribulations of 25 April in their respective capacities, the former had already come within inches of death when, on 25 February, at just after 10.30am, *Agamemnon* came under heavy fire from one of the Ottoman outer forts and was hit amidships on the main derrick-head then through the funnel, killing three men and wounding nine others. The ship was hit five times in all before steaming out of range ten minutes later.

A fortnight later on 7 March *Agamemnon* was once again subjected to heavy fire, this time from one of the Narrows' forts, though, as Denham recorded, 'No casualties at all for us today, and though it was impossible to estimate how much they fired, it must have been a good lot more than 100 shots. We were not sorry when it was over for we had extraordinary good luck not being seriously hit.' He noted, however, a 'hole in the upper deck a yard square'.

Eleven days after that, on 18 March, 'a day to be remembered with regret by the Allied Squadron out here and by the Navy in general', Denham was a front-row witness to what might be regarded in retrospect, as the hours which finally marked – or should have done so due to subsequent dithering, militarily and politically – the beginning of the end of the Anglo-French campaign.

Three Allied battleships, *Bouvet*, *Irresistible* and *Ocean*, were sunk by mines – laid ten days earlier under cover of darkness by a small Turkish sweeper, *Nusret* – resulting in 700 casualties, while Denham recorded at least eleven, mostly howitzer, hits on *Agamemnon* completely wrecking its capstan, two 12-pounders, a motor bollard and after funnel.

As a result of this catastrophic action, what had been first planned as purely a naval operation to force the Narrows in order, as Churchill hoped, to control the Mediterranean–Black Sea supply route, relieve pressure on the Russian army in the Caucasus and encourage Bulgaria and Romania to join the Allies, was now abandoned in favour of military invasion.

However, such lofty and strategic considerations were surely far from the minds of the three young midshipmen as they, separately, converged on Cape Helles in the early hours of that fateful Sunday in late April.

Indeed, the prospect of hazardous front line service must certainly have been the very furthest thing from his mind when, six years earlier, in a letter to his Uncle Drew dated 20 May 1909, George wrote politely: 'I am writing to thank you for the fishing line and hooks. I am very pleased with them. I also want to thank you for all the kindness shown me when I have been at Grimsby and when at home I have always been treated with kindness and well received at your house. And please thank Aunt Eleanor for me …'

If there seems to be a distinct sense of finality about this missive then this all becomes much clearer in the next sentence as George goes on to explain, 'I join my ship, the *Indian Empire*, on Monday and the time draws close.'

SV *Indian Empire*, a 1738-tonne three-masted, cargo-carrying, barque, was constructed in 1896 for owners Duncan, George & Co (Empire Line) by the distinguished Scottish ship-builders, John Reid & Co of the East, the Glen and Newark yards of Port Glasgow. A few years before *Indian Empire* came off the slipway, Reid built the America's Cup challenger *Galatea* (that proved unsuccessful in its bid) and during the same decade was also responsible for the *British Isles*, the largest full-rigged steel ship of its day.

George was just fourteen and a half when, on 24 May 1909, he was one of six apprentices among a crew of fifty-four under the command of its Master, Captain George Perkins Ward, a Devon man, as he climbed aboard the *Indian Empire* in Liverpool's Queen's Dock. This signalled the start of a seagoing life, which would take him more than once round the world, and include a series of near-fatal adventures, across the next nine years in peacetime then in war.

For an enterprising youngster whose principal travel had to date been limited to holidaying between London and Grimsby, the two-year plus itinerary ahead of him must by comparison have seemed almost fantastical, not to say a shade daunting. From Liverpool to

Durban, then back up the East Africa coast to Delagoa Bay (now Maputo Bay) in Mozambique. Thence east and south to Adelaide in South Australia, on to New South Wales, across the Pacific to Taltal on Chile's west coast, continuing round the Horn to Cape Town, back to Adelaide, points west via the Cape of Good Hope to St Helena in the Atlantic and finally, just under 4,000 nautical miles later, back north into Falmouth.

A little over a month after setting sail, George and *Indian Empire* enjoyed their first excitement when a stowaway, one William Joyce, was discovered on board. According to the official ship's log, 'he said he could not get employment and had to live somehow as British seamen were being crowded out by foreigners'. Towards the end of August, at Durban, the incorrigible Joyce is recorded as having 'left the ship and is presumed to have stowed away on the barque *Johanna* of London that sailed alongside'.

Shortly before Christmas at Newcastle, New South Wales, another seaman, John Fraser, caused something of a stir when he was found absent without leave followed, the next day, by being 'laid up off duty from the effects of drink'. The case seems to have been sufficiently serious for Fraser to be hauled up before the deputy stipendiary magistrate in the seaside town at the mouth of the Hunter River where he was convicted and imprisoned for a month with hard labour at the notorious Maitland Gaol about 20 miles inland. He also had to pay costs of £1 7s. The log notes Fraser was 'paid off by mutual consent' on 15 January 1910.

George's first watery brush with death came almost exactly a month later when *Indian Empire* was negotiating the Hunter River near Newcastle. As the ship was being moved, its overhead gear managed somehow to tangle with the spars on the sails of another vessel close by.

Around 9am, George and a fellow apprentice climbed quickly up their rigging to try and clear the obstruction. George suddenly slipped and plummeted 20ft into the river in the course of which he struck the rail with his ankle before falling between his ship and the Italian barque *Enrichetta*. After touching bottom, George struggled back up to the surface but it took a daring rescue act by *Indian Empire*'s Second Mate, Francis Moran, who dived in clutching a rope and helped drag him out of the busy waterway. 'Drury [*sic*] was hauled aboard suffering from bruises and shock,' the log noted.

A newspaper later reported that when George was back on board, he 'cheerfully assured' Captain Ward, 'I don't think there's much the matter with me, sir.' However, a rather more concerned local medic, Dr Eames, ordered him to the city hospital to have his injured ankle properly treated. 'During his stay at the hospital,' the same newspaper trilled, 'he became a great favourite with all the visiting ladies at the institution.'

Moran would, in due course, receive the Royal Humane Society's life-saving award (as well as, on his return to England, a presentation from a grateful Thomas Drewry, who once again would reward one of George's saviours). That August he was also promoted to acting first mate.

The following August, as *Indian Empire* was sailing back home from Adelaide via St Helena, the log recorded the following: 'In consequence of a long passage, 170 days, caused by an abnormal amount of contrary winds and the marine growth on the ship's bottom. After calling at St Helena for provisions and being supplied by [name indecipherable] with a piece of salt meat which proved to be rotten and uneatable although £7 10s was charged for the same, the following have not been supplied to crew inc milk, jam, pickles, syrup – half a pound of tinned meat daily instead of the full allowance of ¾ lb. Compensation to crew of £1 10s per man.'

Indian Empire finally pulled into Falmouth on 26 September 1911, 800 days after leaving Liverpool. A little over six weeks later, on 7 December, 17-year-old George, now under the command of Captain Alexander Isaac, a Riga-born 40-year-old, and with *Indian Empire* having changed ownership from Duncan, George & Co to the London-based firm of Cook & Dundee, set sail again, this time from

Cardiff. Ahead was a voyage of more than 5,500 nautical miles, around Cape Horn and on to the Chilean port city of Mejillones, high up the country's Pacific coast several hours north of the capital, Santiago.

Three months in, on 9 March 1912, having just rounded the infamous Cape but still nearly 2,000 miles shy of her destination, *Indian Empire* was struggling in rough seas with a fierce wind blowing when her steering gear, specifically the rudder, began to falter. The ship became partly disabled and was proving difficult to manage.

When land was sighted, the danger of being driven ashore was so great due to the growing fury of the storm that Captain Isaac decided to bring the head of the vessel more directly into the wind and aim into what appeared to be a little curve of land before finally running *Indian Empire,* with its crew of nine seamen and five apprentices, youngest of whom was 15, on to the nearest stony beach. It so happened, George's father later told newspapers, that the bay was full of kelp which made the water 'practically smooth, otherwise not a single man would have been able to land'.

This, they later discovered, was Hermit Island – just nine miles west of Cape Horn – one of a small chain of Islands off Tierra del Fuego at the southernmost tip of South America, whose only claim to fame before this unplanned stopover was that they had been visited eighty years earlier by Charles Darwin on his *Beagle* voyage.

After getting ashore the crew found themselves in a land of bog and stone – 'an uninhabited and desolate' place, a newspaper would describe it – with no obvious cover of any sort. With heavy rain driving down, a temporary shelter was erected where the men stood or crouched through that first night.

In the morning it was found that through a hole in her bows, the ship had taken on water, which meant the entire after portion was submerged. It was clear now that *Indian Empire* was a shipwreck. Most of the provisions had been rendered useless and the men were only able to recover a small portion of their belongings.

Heavy rain continued for seven solid days and nights on the hapless crew, who did at least successfully manage to construct a more stable shelter using the ship's sails. Less successful was an attempt to cross bog and stone in order to try and discover any more hospitable corner of this benighted isle.

A few biscuits had been saved from the wreck along with a large undamaged stock of salt beef, which were then carefully rationed out by Captain Isaac. As well as fishing, the men also gathered clams and shellfish along with a plant later described as 'a sort of cabbage'. At the end of a week in which they were restricted to just two meals a day, it was quickly apparent that supplies were now running dangerously low. Captain Isaac realized that urgent action was necessary, picked a crew of seven men and set off in a lifeboat – another of the stricken *Indian Empire*'s more crucial legacies – in search of help.

At the end of the next week, having been sixteen days on the island, the remaining crew were now reduced almost to despair by their increasingly meagre diet and the fear they had seen the last of their other shipmates. Then gloom turned to joy as they suddenly spotted a launch that had been swiftly dispatched from the Chilean convict settlement at Begal which the lifeboat party had eventually reached.

The journey to Begal took three days and was increasingly uncomfortable as the launch was so small the men had to stand, crammed like upright sardines, for much of its duration. Once at Begal, the next two nights' stay on a convict hulk was luxury by comparison. From Begal the crew was transferred, first, by a Chilean gunboat, *Piedra Buena*, to Punta Arenas, thence back to Liverpool and home on the British liner SS *Oropesa*, of the Pacific Steam Navigation Company, which would later serve as an armed merchant cruiser with the French Navy.

The public first heard, briefly, of George and his shipmates' rescue in the papers on 10 April, a little over a month after *Indian Empire* had foundered on Hermit Island. Five days later came the shattering news of an altogether more shocking ocean disaster – the sinking of RMS *Titanic* in the North Atlantic with the loss of more than 1,500 lives.

The full story of George's ordeal – a 'Thrilling Shipwreck Experience', according to the *Derry Journal*, with, happily, no loss of life – finally made the papers in May.

> *None of the crew had suffered from illness and all reported themselves in excellent health. The cabin boy was downcast, however. 'They have been calling me "Jonah" again,' he said. 'It was my first voyage.'*
>   *'And you won't go to sea again?'*
>   *'Yes, I will, as soon as I can get a ship,' he said.*

Sadly, the cabin boy remains anonymous however the same sort of stiff-upper-lip determination evidently infused George as well for, just a month or so after returning from South America, and still short of his eighteenth birthday, he was to be found registered as an employee of his father's company, P&O, with the rank of fifth officer (uncertified), on the passenger/cargo liner, the *Palma*.

He was one of twenty-six Europeans, in a predominantly Asian crew, as the Belfast-built ship plied its trade on the India, Far East and, occasionally, Australia, run.

A year later, George was in P&O's seniority list certified as a fourth officer and had also been awarded a certificate of competency as second mate of a foreign-going ship in the Merchant Service. His new ship was *Isis*. Around the same time, he also enlisted as a midshipman in the Royal Naval Reserve, the self-described branch of the Senior Service for professional seafarers.

Isis, with an Anglo–Italian crew of 155, operated a shuttle service between Brindisi in southern Italy and Port Said, at the northern tip of the Suez Canal in Egypt. Built in 1898, she and her sister *Osiris*, boasting a maximum speed of twenty knots, were designed for the express service between the two ports, taking mail and passengers who travelled overland through Europe to save time – four days to Egypt instead of twelve days by the all-sea route.

Known as 'submarines' because they were reputed to submerge off Brindisi and not surface until reaching Egypt, they could, however, scarcely be considered comfortable, despite boasting seventy-four first class berths. The first dozen or so years of service for *Isis* – before George's posting – were not without incident, including a collision with a sailing ship, the loss of a starboard propeller, an on-board fire in one of the mail rooms and a short-lived engine crew revolt.

Then, on 3 August 1914, the day before Britain officially declared war on Germany, 19-year-old George was in Port Said when he, along with 30,000 officers and men of the RNR, was called up for Navy service. He swapped fourth officer for probationary midshipman, and *Isis* for the base, or depot, ship, HMS *Egmont*, at the centre of the Grand Harbour in Malta, 900 miles east of Egypt. In reality *Egmont* was not a ship at all, rather a large bastioned fort used as a Royal Navy military installation, also known as a 'stone frigate'.

Exactly a month later, on 3 September, George's neatly handwritten initials first appear in the 'officer of the watch' column of the shipping logs for HMS *Hussar* which would become his station, on and off, for the next two years. Launched as a torpedo gunboat in 1894, *Hussar* first served in the Mediterranean between 1896 and 1905 before being used, principally, for fishery protection. In 1907 *Hussar* had her armament removed while being converted into the yacht and despatch vessel for the Royal Navy's Commander-in-Chief Mediterranean, Sir Charles Drury. At the outbreak of war, she, like many other such former gunboats, was re-fitted out as a minesweeper.

For the next six months or so, *Hussar* and George's seagoing existence was, if you believe the logs, an uneventful series of mainly Aegean-based patrols between Salonika (now Thessaloniki) and Dedeagach (Alexandropouli) in the north to Syra (Syros) in the Cyclades with occasional diversions to Athens, Alexandria, Brindisi, Malta and Marseilles.

As the Allied casualty count began to mount closer to home on the Western Front, George's duties throughout this period included general ship's maintenance, taking on coal, rifle drill, target practice and even, rather more intriguingly, 'waling' – presumably whaling – with a daily haul recorded as between 100 and 135 tons. Apart from his occasional 'watch' initials, the only other log reference to George was when he and some others 'donned diving dress and exercised monthly diving dip' in a sea that would at that time of year still have been decidedly chilly.

Then, at 8.30pm on 4 March 1915, Commander Unwin was piped aboard *Hussar* as her new captain. A few days later *Hussar* docked at Mudros to begin preparations for the April landings.

On 18 April, exactly a week before the 'big adventure' as he described it in his 1923 memoir, *Hard Lying* (a term applied to a special allowance granted to men serving in small craft such as destroyers, torpedo boats and trawlers), Captain L.B. Weldon MC rowed over by dinghy – himself stroke and his Greek cook, bow – to visit Rear Admiral Wemyss, Governor of Mudros, who was aboard his yacht, *Imogene*.

Business concluded, Captain Weldon returned on deck where, he wrote: 'I found a "Snotty" at the top of the gangway, who saluted and politely asked me if he could call a boat for me. I said "yes", of course. Then, looking round, he told me my boat wasn't there. So I pointed to the dinghy with our greasy old cook in it. The "Snotty's" face was a picture as he watched me take off my tunic and pull away. He naturally thought I had come in some naval boat. This "Snotty's" name was Drewry and later on he won a VC at Gallipoli.'

'*The destination will be the Mediterranean. The orders specify Gibraltar, and thence to the Eastern Mediterranean for operations against the Turks.*'
   Godden whistled. 'Gallipoli, by God!'
   Royston-Jones pursed his lips. 'As you put it, Commander, Gallipoli.'
                                    Douglas Reeman, *HMS Saracen*

Chapter 4

V Beach, 25 April (contd.)

One moment it had been early morning in a peaceful country, with thoughts or smells of cows and hay and milk; and the next, while the boats were just twenty yards from the shore, the blue sea round each boat was turning red. Is there anything more horrible than to see men wading through water waist-high under heavy fire? You see where each bullet hits the water, which, like a nightmare, holds back the man for the next shot, which will not miss.

Lieutenant Commander Josiah Wedgwood DSO MP

Despite everything that would transpire so brutally over the next twenty-four hours or so, George could hardly contain his youthful excitement when he tried to describe the extraordinary scene to his father. His letter was dated 12 May, just seventeen days after we last left him shortly before dawn heading for Cape Helles in the steam hopper *Argyle* as shell from the four 12-inch guns of HMS *Albion* rained noisily over him.

'Dad, it was glorious!' he enthused, 'Dozens of ships. Battleships, cruisers, destroyers and transports. The morning mist lay on the land, which seemed to be a mass of fire and smoke as the ships raked it with shell. Straight into the sun past battleships roaring with their 12 inch, the noise was awful and the air full of powder. Shell began to fall around us thick but did not hit us. We were half a mile from the beach and we were told "not yet", so we took a turn round two ships.'

Albion, a further half mile out to seaward, had started its bombardment at 5.04am. A little over twenty-five minutes later, at 5.30am, when the tows were originally scheduled to land, she ceased firing with the curtain of smoke and mist hanging thickly over the shoreline. Then, as the tows were not now making proper headway because of the vagaries of the current, *Albion*, an old pre-dreadnought battleship, began another furious, if, as it transpired, wildly inaccurate onslaught.

'At last,' wrote George, still gung-ho, 'we had the signal at 6am and in we dashed, Unwin on the bridge [of the *River Clyde*] and I at the helm of the hopper with my crew.'

But what, just a half hour after sunrise, actually lay before them, its aspect still barely discernible through the shroud of shell fire, this Ertugrul Cove, officially designated V Beach?

'The configuration ... was that of an amphitheatre,' as described pithily in his diary by Captain Guy Geddes, commander of the Munsters' X Company. 'To the west high cliffs surmounted by Fort No.1 and to the east the fort of Sedd-el-Bahr guarding the western entrance of the mouth of the straits. The radii of this amphitheatre being about 300 yards. A tier of trenches ran just under the crest with three rows of wire entanglements. The wire so thick that no wire cutters as supplied would make any impression. Barbs of 2 inches were spaced every 3 inches on the wire, the standards of iron with spiked tops being set on iron plates set 2 feet into the ground.'

Both forts had been severely blasted by earlier naval bombardment but, as Sir Ian Hamilton would later describe in the first of his retrospective Gallipoli despatches, 'their crumbled walls and the ruined outskirts of the village [*Sedd-el-Bahr*] afforded cover for riflemen, while from the terraced slopes already described the defenders were able to command the open beach, as a stage is overlooked from the balconies of a theatre.'

Above the uppermost jumble of barbed wire, the terrain was pitted with enemy trenches, in one of which four pom-poms (37mm quick-firing guns) were sited. 'In others,' wrote Hamilton, 'were dummy pom-poms to draw fire, while the debris of the shattered buildings on either flank afforded cover and concealment for a number of machine guns, which brought a cross-fire to bear on the ground already swept by rifle fire from the ridge.'

Or, as John Masefield would summarise more succinctly, 'modern defence could not ask for a more perfect site'.

Mind you, it wasn't as though the Allies weren't aware of the general terrain for, in February and March, there had been four separate, albeit minor, forays at Sedd-el-Bahr by the Royal Navy. However, that had naturally given the Turkish defenders 'a six-week opportunity to practise a response to any likely landings over and over again to get their arcs of fire right, get their fire discipline correct, and put out the wire', as explained to me by Clive Harris, Gallipoli expert and battlefield guide.

'There were some forms of exploding mines beneath the waterline – not like landmines as we know it – but with a sort of tripwire fuse. And, of course, the big problem with V Beach is that for our soldiers, there is no cover. There was the tiny little spithead – and there's a famous photo of the Munsters sheltering by it. What we don't know is what time of day it was taken, whether it was early the next morning, or soon as the attack started or late on in the day,' he added.

Yet all remained eerily silent, mostly obscured and still seemingly unthreatening from the shore as George and Unwin, in their respective vessels, along with an array of small tow boats, some twenty in all packed with thirty-six Dublins in each, edged closer and closer to their objective.

The idea had been for the *River Clyde* to follow the tows in but in the melee of craft, as veiled in smoke and mist as the shoreline, it became apparent that the collier had somehow edged ahead which might seriously confuse the impending egress if beached first. Unwin was all for carrying on but the senior army officers at his side made it clear they should stick to the original plan and he should delay the *River Clyde*'s approach.

However, notes historian Nigel Steel, 'It was impossible for the *River Clyde* to come to a halt without the danger of fouling the lines towing the hopper and the lighters. So, instead, Unwin steered a circle through the crowded waters and skilfully passed between two destroyers of the mine sweeping flotilla, one of which had to release her sweeping wire at the last moment as the *River Clyde* passed over.

'The result of this drastic manoeuvre was a significant loss of speed and consequently of momentum. It had been hoped that the *River Clyde* would run at the shore with a speed of about nine knots and by doing so would drive herself well inland. But because of the loss in speed, when the circle was complete and she finally began her second approach, she was actually only able to build up to five knots and the eventual impact was much lighter than the soldiers on board were expecting.'

Despite Unwin's adroit navigation, the ship still remained slightly ahead of the tows but it was now simply too late to reverse the situation.

According to Lieutenant Colonel Williams' diary, which he jotted on the bridge of the *River Clyde* almost minute by minute:

'6.22am Ran smoothly ashore without a tremor. No opposition. We shall land unopposed.

'6.25am Tows within a few yards of shore...'

As the first boats touched bottom, the fearful silence was suddenly shattered. 'Hell broke loose', Williams now scribbled, with uncharacteristic emotion. In that instant, a fusillade of rifle, pom-pom fire and possibly machine-gun too, began to hail down on the troops from the heights, while howitzer batteries further inland dealt deadly shrapnel.

'Then the fun began', George wrote, before observing in one stark sentence, shocking in its brevity, 'the soldiers jumped out as the boats beached and they died, almost all of them wiped out with the boats' crews'.

'The fun'? It began, it was said, with a single shot before becoming what was variously described as 'a continuous roar ... the placid water off the beach was hissing with bullets' (Captain Eric Bush) and, yet more vividly, 'a tornado of fire ... lashing the calm water of the bay with a thousand whips' (Brigadier General Aspinall-Oglander).

It is estimated that just 300 of the 700 troops in that first wave reached the shore, many of them wounded, as they sought the only cover available from this onslaught, a low, sandy escarpment, some 4ft or so high, which ran along almost the length of the beach. 'That lucky ledge of sand', as it was characterized in the campaign's official history, helped spare many lives.

Gruelling, even dispiriting, as it must have been to witness at such proximity the ongoing carnage amid a deafening soundscape – it was reckoned that the Turks were firing between 5,000 and 12,000 shots a minute during that blitz – George still had a huge job to do.

The plan was that once the *River Clyde* had run aground, the *Argyle* should move ahead on the port side pulling at least, ideally, two of the three available lighters into position to form a bridge from the ship to the actual beach. The best laid plan …

According to an unreliable account by Colonel Hans Kannengiesser Pasha, who was on the staff of the German Commander, General Liman von Sanders, 'the ship did not stop, but drove into the arena and crashed at full speed against the beach so that the bows crumpled. The propeller churned sand and water madly astern forcing the ship still further ashore. The Turks looked on with astonishment.'

'Directly we took the beach,' Unwin wrote later, 'I rushed to the side of the bridge to see how the hopper was getting on and was horrified to see Drewry hacking at the tow rope with an axe. I had told him only to put the eye over the bollard as, of course, when we struck, the tow would slacken and all he had to do was lift it off the bollard. When he did get free, she [*the Argyle*] sheared off to port and was of no further use except as a death trap to a lot of men who were trying to land in boats …'

According to George: 'We had a line from the stern of the hopper to the lighters and this we tried to haul in, the hardest haul I've ever tried. Then the Capt appeared on the lighters and the steam pinnace took hold of the lighters and plucked them in until she could go no closer. Instead of joining up to the hopper the Capt decided to make the connection with a spit of rock on the other bow. Seeing this we let go our rope and Samson and I tried to put a brow [*a sort of gangplank*] out over the bow.' However, 'the Greeks had run below ...'

What had actually happened, noted Stephen Snelling, was that 'rather than pulling ahead as intended, the *Argyle* had actually gone into reverse before suddenly lurching to port at right angles to the *River Clyde* (which, in any case, had grounded 'a little too far to the eastward,' confessed Unwin). Either by accident or design, the Greek crew had effectively sabotaged the hopper's mission. Then, with bullets falling like hail, they had, in Samson's words, 'bolted down into the engine-room'.

Most likely is that the Greeks, who reasonably felt this wasn't their war at all, had simply tried to retreat as rapidly as possible from the unfolding horror before them as swiftly as they could; this, despite the fact that, as Unwin confided later, they 'had begged me to be allowed to come'.

The situation was disintegrating by the minute. With the Greeks out of the picture, George realized that he and Samson couldn't deploy the brow on their own so he told the seaman to try and shelter from the barrage.

'I jumped over the bow and waded ashore. Meeting a soldier wounded in the water, we (I & another soldier from a boat) tried to carry him ashore but he was again shot in our arms, his neck in two pieces nearly. So we left him and I ran along the beach towards the spit. I threw away my revolver, coat & hat and waded out to the Captain.

'He was in the water with a man named Williams [Able Seaman Williams] wading and towing the lighters towards the spit. I gave a pull for a few minutes and then climbed aboard the lighters. The Captain, still in the water, sang out for more rope. So I went on board and brought a rope down with the help of a man called Ellard [*a seaman volunteer from Hussar*].'

Nigel Steel: 'Once Unwin had manoeuvred the two lighters into position in front of the *River Clyde*, he then discovered that there was nothing suitable on the shore near the spit of rocks to which they could be secured whilst the soldiers disembarked.

'Seeing no immediate alternative, he decided to wind the line from the lighters round himself and then submerge in the water up to his shoulders, using his own body as a fixing point. Williams, seeing this, then further added his own weight to the line to secure it and once this was done Unwin shouted to Tizard on the *River Clyde* that the landing could begin.'

Lieutenant Colonel Henry Tizard was the commanding officer of the Munsters.

Shortly after 7am, what had been the 'hell' of half an hour earlier was, from the moment the 'Trojan Horse', as the *River Clyde* was dubbed by the Turks, started to disgorge its human cargo, about to be superseded by something altogether more terrible. The scene all too quickly would begin to resemble 'a cross between a slaughterhouse and a cemetery' (Douglas Reeman) as much of the enemy fire now became firmly and fatally concentrated on the grounded collier, its open ports and gangplanks.

As the men tried to run ashore, many were immediately cut down before they reached the beach, some were shot in shallow water, others, weighed down by their heavy backpacks, drowned, or were killed by sniper fire where they stood on board, and yet more were about to perish by shell while still crouched in their holds.

Admiral (then Commodore) Roger Keyes in his memoir, *The Fight for Gallipoli*, provided graphic eyewitness as he observed from on board the battleship, HMS *Queen Elizabeth*, Hamilton's flagship:

'As the visibility improved we could see clearly that the attack was being most bloodily held up. It was a ghastly sight to watch from a position of absolute safety. The foreshore was strewn with dead bodies and wreckage of stranded boats. The sea was whipped up by bullets. Between the *River Clyde* and the shore we could see men struggling up to their shoulders in the sea; others lying under the shelter of a ridge in the sand, to move from which meant certain death from machine guns which could not be located from the covering ships.'

It appeared to Keyes that Unwin and George, among others, seemed 'to bear charmed lives [as they] worked incessantly under a murderous fire to restore communication with the shore; the midshipmen swimming to and fro with lines to connect the lighters and haul them into position.'

Some were more charmed than others. Williams was still in the water with Unwin when he was hit by a shell, which had been fired from the Asia side of the Straits. 'As we reached the end of the lighters,' wrote George. 'the Capt was wading towards us carrying Williams, we pulled him on to the lighter and Ellard carried him on board the ship on his shoulders, but he spoilt the act by not coming down again.' Williams, however, had died in his Captain's arms.

A Boer War and Boxer Rebellion veteran, 35-year-old Williams should never have been in that line of fire in the first place but had somehow managed to talk his way on to the *River Clyde* assignment. Unwin would later describe him as the bravest man he ever knew.

Soldiers had been coming ashore from the Clyde *for over half an hour, stumbling half-heartedly over the rubble of men and equipment strewn in the sea and on the shingle. Shoulders bent against the rain, they said no more than the occasional swear word as barbed wire caught their hands and wounded men their feet. They were like the dark ghosts of the men who had left a mere twenty-four hours earlier ... amidst flags, bands and cheering.*

Rachel Billington, *Glory*

Now, at this moment, with Unwin frozen and exhausted to the point of collapse, lighters drifting, and bodies piling up, George's defining role in the action was at hand.

'Got a rope from the lighter to the spit and then with difficulty I hauled the Capt onto the lighter. He was nearly done and I was alone.

He went inboard and the Doctor had rather a job with him. All this time shells were falling all around us and into the ship, one hitting the casing of one boiler but doing no further damage. Several men were killed by two shells in No.4 hold,' he continued, matter-of-factly.

'I stayed on the lighters and tried to keep the men going ashore but it was murder and soon the first lighter was covered with dead and wounded, and the spit was awful, the sea round it for some yards was red.'

Here was confirmation of one of the campaign's most infamous sights – the sea off V Beach 'running red with blood'. It would be regularly noted in other Allied, as well as in Turkish, accounts of the landing.

Air Commodore Charles Rumney Samson, one-time midshipman and naval aviation pioneer, recalled in a 1930 memoir, *Fights and Flights* as he flew over Sedd-el-Bahr in his biplane, 'the sea for a distance of about 50 yards from the beach was absolutely red with blood, a horrible sight to see'. One theory that, from the air, the intrepid aviator might have mistaken seaweed for blood, seems unlikely.

Perhaps the most graphic account of them all came from Major Mahmut, a Balkan Wars veteran, who was commanding the Ottoman's 3rd Battalion, 26th Regiment. Quoted by historian Peter Hart, he declared: 'The fire changed the colour of the sea with the blood from the bodies of the enemy – a sea whose colour had remained the same for years.

'Shells and machine-gun bullets fell ceaselessly at the points where rifle fire was observed, but in spite of this, heavy fire was opened from all our trenches. In a vain attempt to save their lives, the enemy threw themselves from the boats into the sea. The shore became full of enemy corpses, like a shoal of fish.'

Blood not just in the sea but also on the beach as George observed troops who once ashore were 'little better off for they were picked off, many of them before they could dig themselves in'.

The almost suicidal flow from the ship had stopped as George 'ran on board into the No.1 [hold] and saw an awful sight. Dead and dying lay around the ports where their curiosity had led them. I went up to the saloon and saw the Capt being rubbed down. He murmured something about the third lighter so I went down again and in a few minutes a picket boat came along the starboard side and gave the reserve lighter a push that sent it as far as the hopper.'

By this time, the lighters had begun to drift away from the spit when suddenly, 'a piece of shrapnel hit me on the head knocking me down for a second or two and covering me with blood'. With George now was Lieutenant Tony Morse of HMS *Cornwallis*, a pre-dreadnought battleship, which had enjoyed the distinction of firing the first shells of the Dardanelles campaign a little over two months earlier on 15 February. It was now around 8am.

Morse was the senior officer with a 38-strong party from *Cornwallis* divided into four boats, which were being towed in shore by a steam pinnace from *Albion*. The contingent included five midshipmen, most notably 18-year-old Wilfred St Aubyn Malleson, whose illustrious name would, for many, become forever bracketed with George's.

Meanwhile, George himself needed some medical attention for his head wound as he and Morse made their lighter fast to the hopper. He went below where 'a Tommy put a scarf around my head and I went up again'.

It was imperative that the lighters should be properly secured together so, apparently still oblivious of the ceaseless rain of shells, George, his head now perfunctorily bandaged, jumped back into the sea clasping a rope and began to swim towards the other lighters, which were drifting dangerously below the bows of the *River Clyde*.

'But,' George wrote, 'the rope was not long enough and I was stuck in the middle. I sang out to Mid. Malleson to throw me a line, but he had no line except the one that had originally kept the lighters to the spit. He stood up and hauled this line in (almost half a coil) and then, as I drifted away he swam towards the lighter I had left and made it alright.' Courage upon courage, in full view of the enemy.

Like Unwin earlier, George was near collapse – 'rather played out', as he described it, diffidently – but somehow managed to get back to ship, clambering with some difficulty across the lighters before getting on board where 'the Doctor [Burrowes Kelly] dressed my head and rubbed me down. I was awfully cold'. Unwin, now feeling 'alright again' watched as 'they brought Drewry in. He told me a bullet had grazed his forehead, a very near thing. They bound him up, and he was soon about again.'

However, wrote George, Dr Kelly 'would not let me get up, and I had to lay down and listen to the din'. Malleson, having completed the job George had started, soon joined him on the ship.

The 'din' they both must have heard was, according to Stephen Snelling, 'almost certainly the renewed attempt to get men ashore from the *River Clyde*. So heavy were the losses among a third company of the Munsters that the disembarkment was once again suspended. Orders were issued to the troops to "hold on and wait". In truth there was little else they could do.'

However, that wasn't going to stop Unwin who was determined to return to the fray. He recalled: 'As I had no uniform with me I got into a white shirt and flannel trousers and went out on to the hopper to see if I could do any good. I don't think I did but with the help of an old merchant seaman, he looked at least 70, and a boy, I got a line out, but I don't think it was ever used.'

The sudden re-appearance of the doughty commander was at least good for morale, it seems, for, as George recorded, a loud cheer went up. Looking out of the port, he saw Unwin 'standing on the hopper in white clothes. A line had carried away and by himself he had fixed it,' he added, admiringly.

With that, George finally followed doctor's orders, lay down and somehow fell asleep, despite the continuing pounding of the ship from both shores often with fatal consequences for some of the men still inside. Waking some hours later, at 3pm, he learned that the hopper's bow 'had swung around and there was no connection with the shore. I got up and found nothing was going to be done until dark. At dusk the firing seemed to cease, and the connection was made to the spit again.'

Despite having carried out the action that would form the basis of his subsequent VC citation, George's day was still far from done. But first he was to discover something of what had transpired while he was still asleep, notably that the Captain, who had been hit in the face and neck by fragments of a bullet from a ricochet, and one or two volunteers 'had taken seven loads of wounded from the lighters to No.4 hold by the starboard side. A great feat, which everyone is talking about.' Typically, this reflection centred on a man to whom, everyone seemed to agree, George was devoted.

What he would also have learned second-hand but may have been reluctant to impart here because, as he'd note near the end of his missive, 'the censor would tear this up', was the sheer, indiscriminate scale of the slaughter at V Beach, from top brass such as Brigadier General Napier, who was commanding 88 Brigade, his Brigade Major, Captain John Costeker and Lieutenant Colonel Herbert Carington-Smith, senior officer of the Hampshires, down to the humblest foot soldier and seaman, some 2,000 casualties in total.

Neither would George have witnessed the eventual demise of Sub-Lieutenant Tisdall, a part, too, of the original *River Clyde* expedition, who had spent hours in the morning rescuing wounded off the rocks while under heavy fire. On 6 May Tisdall was with his platoon, finally on dry land, when he was shot through the chest and died, about four miles inland from V Beach.

Around 8pm, an hour after sunset, and with enemy fire having subsided, the troops began to make for the beach again while George organized a party of men to retrieve more wounded from the hopper and the lighters and transfer them to a trawler 'laying under our quarter. An awful job, they had not been dressed at all and some of the poor devils were in an awful state. I never knew that blood smelt so strong before.'

But the onset of night certainly didn't spell an end to the day's bloody battle. Some time after 11.30pm, as Sunday began to turn into Monday, the Turks started firing again. George: 'They gave us an awful doing, shell, shrapnel and every other nasty thing. But everyone laid low and little harm was done.' The barrage finally ended, he reckoned, around 2am.

The rest of George's letter to his father comprised a series of his observations about some of the events that took place in and around V Beach on 26 April, beginning with, 'all through the night the village [*Sedd-el-Behr*] was burning and gave us too much light to be pleasant. In the morning our people worked up the right and took the fort and then worked slowly into the village and took it house by house.'

Later in the day, from the *River Clyde*, George witnessed Colonel Doughty-Wylie leading what turned out to be a successful charge to take the old fort atop the much-vaunted Hill 141 while losing his life and earning a posthumous VC in the process – 'all this we saw quite plainly from the ship'. He also paid tribute to 'Geordie' Samson – 'my hopper man who did very well on the Sunday afternoon' – noting that on the Monday, 'he was severely wounded while sniping from the foredeck of the ship'.

His concluding remarks seem almost anti-climactic by comparison with the almost unimaginable horrors of the preceding thirty-six hours. He told his father how he'd run ashore across the spit and took a photo from the beach, 'but the bullets began to fly so I ran back'. Then, that evening, 'a dog frightened one Tommy. He fired at it and so did the rest for nearly an hour.'

The letter ends by offering some more casual observations as George awaited his imminent recall to duties on HMS *Hussar*: 'Ten minutes walk and I can see the men in our trenches. In the Straits I can see the enemy's shell falling round our ships and always the roar of guns goes on. We have been bombarded by aeroplanes, but no damage done. I've seen a German chased by two of our planes ...'

Ends? Well, not exactly, for the letter actually concludes, at times tantalisingly, with the following:

'By next mail I hope to send you some photos taken here. Some of them I believe will be of interest and I'm wondering if you could send them to the papers for me?

As we came away I received a letter from the Company about the bonus to be given. This I have lost, also the forms for the difference of pay. Could you speak to Mr [*indecipherable*] in our department and see if he would fix it for me?

The Admiral sent for me on the 28th and gave me a shift of clean clothes and the use of his bath. Some luck.

There is lots yet I could tell you but I must not so will send my love and close.

Best of health.

Your affectionate son

George'

The 'Company' was, of course, P&O. This missive may have been dated less than three weeks after the hell of V Beach, but it was obvious that George wasn't sufficiently traumatised at the time to neglect attending to the promise of back pay.

As for the 'Admiral' and his generosity, one suspects this had to be 'Rosy' Wemyss, who had championed the *River Clyde* experiment from the outset. The blessed 'bath' would therefore have been aboard his flagship, *Euryalus*.

The letter also contained a couple of crude sketches; one, an outline of the *River Clyde* showing the position of the three lighters; the other a rough map of V Beach and its outlying features. George referred to photos he had taken – and would do so again in his later letters – but my research yielded nothing on that score.

Three days after the landings, George would, according to Snelling's book about the Gallipoli VCs, have been seen touring the ruined village of Sedd-el-Bahr where he fainted at the sight of so many Turkish and British bodies. 'Never afterwards would he photograph anywhere near Sedd-el-Bahr', recorded Surgeon Burrowes Kelly.

By the time George returned to his ship, Winston Churchill, First Lord of the Admiralty, instigator and principal architect of the Dardanelles campaign, was probably one of the first back home to have been made aware of the midshipman's courage thanks to a two-part letter, dated 25 and 26 April, from his fellow parliamentarian, Lieutenant Colonel Wedgwood, who was commanding the machine guns on the *River Clyde*.

Wedgwood, badly wounded eleven days later at the Second Battle of Krithia, began his letter, 'Dear Churchill, This ought to be a most interesting letter if it is ever finished, for we are on the wreck ship ...' before going on to describe in some graphic detail the bloodbath that ensued in the battle for V Beach shortly after dawn.

Then, he went on, 'let me tell you of the deeds of heroism I witnessed. It is pleasanter, and I could not have believed them possible. Midshipman Drury [sic] of the *Clyde* swam to the hopper, was wounded in the head, got a line off the hopper and got somehow back to the ship with it,' followed by an account of Unwin's and several others' courage.

When later that same year Wedgwood published his short memoir of the action, George, his surname misspelling still intact, was not forgotten: 'There, now, was Midshipman Drury swimming to the lighter which had broken loose, with a line in his mouth and a wound in his head. If ever a boy deserved his VC that lad did.'

For his part, Churchill would, in his 1933 part work on the Great War, compiled during his so-called 'Wilderness Years', refer only briefly to V Beach. He paid this tribute: 'Commander Unwin and the small naval staff responsible for fixing the lighters, and, indeed, for the plan of using the *River Clyde*, persevered in their endeavours to secure their lighters and lay down gangways unremittingly in the deadly storm, while others struggled with unsurpassed heroism to save the drowning and dying or to make their way armed to the shore.'

It is perhaps interesting now to speculate whether George, despite his youth and comparative inexperience, ever contemplated, at the time or even in the few years left to him that followed, the essential folly of his captain's 'Wooden Horse' experiment.

According to Peter Hart: 'The Trojans of legend had no idea what lay within the "gift" left them by the Greeks; that indeed was the whole point. At V Beach the Turks could plainly see the gangways, they knew what would happen when the ship ran aground and they had more than enough time to train their rifles on the exit ports.'

Nigel Steel underlined the point: 'In devising the *River Clyde*, Unwin had inadvertently created one of the most difficult of military positions, a defile which opened at close range onto an entrenched enemy position. The narrowness of the *River Clyde*'s pontoon link forced the disembarking soldiers to collect together at exactly the point where the enemy's fire was strongest.' The result was that more than half of the officers and men who left the ship were either killed or wounded.

As for Unwin, he remained for the most part unapologetic. In his letter to Wemyss, he wrote: 'In all accounts I have read of the *River Clyde* it has always been stated that owing to the current I beached the ship in the wrong place. I beached the ship exactly where I intended to, and where you ordered me to.

'The picturesque part of my show was spoilt by the failure of the hopper to continue my line, a perfectly simple thing to do. Some years later I was walking in the VC procession to Buckingham Palace with ['Geordie'] Samson next to me. I said "Samson, I never said anything at the time, but why did the hopper go adrift like she did?" He said, "It was them bloody Greeks. As soon as the firing began they went full speed astern." This, of course, would account for it.'

However, Unwin went on to admit 'my only one real mistake', that he should have cut the exit 'in the extreme eyes of the ship. This would have saved all the staging that I had to put in, but there would still have to be an exit and on that the Turks would have concentrated just the same with the same result, the enfilading of the troops inside.'

He also added, 'Speaking after the event, I think we should have run in an hour before dawn, or possibly two hours then we could have got all the troops ashore before the enemy could distinguish our exit. What I do claim is that the old *River Clyde* saved hundreds of lives that would have inevitably been lost had the troops she carried landed, or tried to land, in boats, for they would have all been killed.'

Sir Ian Hamilton required no retrospect to state baldly in his diary at the time, 'this V Beach business is the blot. Sedd-el-Bahr was supposed to be the softest landing of the lot, as it was the best harbour and seemed to lie specially at the mercy of the big guns of the fleet. Would that we had left it severely alone and had landed a big force at Morto Bay [*a large inlet to the east of Sedd-el-Bahr above the Cape*] whence we could have forced the Sedd-el-Bahr Turks to fall back.'

However, Hamilton re-assured himself, and whatever the verdict of history on the folly or otherwise of the campaign, of this there surely remains no argument: 'Whatever happens to us here, we are bound to win glory.'

Major (then Captain) Albert Mure was with the 1/5th Royal Scots, part of 88 Brigade, who had been due to land at V Beach in support of the Dublins, Munsters and Hampshires but were diverted to W Beach because the initial attack was held up. Instead, in relative safety, he watched from the deck of a transport as the offensive began.

In a lavish part work about the Great War, published twenty years after the conflict, subtitled *I Was There*, Major Mure recalled the events of 25 April.

Under the headline 'Dauntless in the Face of Death: I saw the heroes of *River Clyde*', he wrote, 'a Turkish officer, our prisoner later, swore by Allah that it was the finest thing he ever saw, and ten times braver than he would have credited of any man, Christian or Mussulman.'

There was a bright moon, and as we saw the pale cliffs of Cape Helles, all, I think, expected each moment a torrent of shells from some obscure quarter. But instead an unearthly stillness brooded over the two bays, and only a Morse lamp blinking at the sweeper suggested that any living thing was there. And there came over the water a strange musty smell, some said it was the smell of the dead, and some the smell of an incinerator; myself I do not know, but it was the smell of the Peninsula for ever, which no man can forget. We disembarked at a pair of rafts by the River Clyde, and stumbled eagerly ashore. And now we were in the very heart of heroic things. Nowhere, I think, was the new soldier plunged so suddenly into the genuine scenes of war as he was at Gallipoli ... we stood, suddenly, on the very sand where, but three weeks before, those hideous machine guns in the cliffs had mown down that astonishing party of April 25, and in that silver stillness it was difficult to believe.

A.P. Herbert, *The Secret Battle*

Chapter 5

For Valour

*You have behaved very well, my good lad, on all occasions in which
your courage and conduct as an officer have been called forth.'*
                                                    Mr Midshipman Easy

It would take almost another four months before the world officially
first learned much more fully of the tumultuous events of 25/26 April
concerning the *River Clyde* and its crew's courageous role in the ill-
fated landing at V Beach. This would be courtesy of a graphic despatch
by Admiral de Robeck posted as a special supplement in *The London
Gazette* of 16 August, albeit fully six weeks after he had initially laid it
all out in a long letter to the Admiralty.

From aboard HMS *Triad*, a chartered yacht which served as De
Robeck's flagship in the Dardanelles, he detailed unflinchingly the
faltering egress from the old collier.

First noting that 'it was anticipated this beach would be the most
difficult to capture,' he went on, 'V Beach was subjected to a heavy
bombardment similarly to W Beach, with the same result, i.e., when
the first trip attempted to land they were met with a murderous fire
from rifle, pom-pom and machine gun, which was not opened till the
boats had cast off from the steamboats.

'A landing on the flanks here was impossible and practically all the
first trip were either killed or wounded, a few managing to find some
slight shelter under a bank on the beach; in several boats all were either
killed or wounded; one boat entirely disappeared, and in another there
were only two survivors. Immediately after the boats had reached the
beach the *River Clyde* was run ashore under a heavy fire rather towards

the eastern end of the beach, where she could form a convenient breakwater during future landing of stores, etc.

'As the *River Clyde* grounded, the lighters which were to form the bridge to the shore were run out ahead of the collier, but unfortunately they failed to reach their proper stations and a gap was left between two lighters over which it was impossible for men to cross; some attempted to land by jumping from the lighter which was in position into the sea and wading ashore; this method proved too costly, the lighter being soon heaped with dead and the disembarkation was ordered to cease.'

Then, as if somehow to stem this relentless recitation of pending disaster, he spelt out more specifically the extraordinary bravery and derring-do amid the bloody chaos, of, among many others, Commander Unwin and his younger shipmates, Drewry, Samson and Williams, concluding, with typical British understatement: 'During this period many heroic deeds were performed in rescuing wounded men in the water.'

There followed the roll-call of naval awards 'the King has been graciously pleased to approve', glowingly laid out, name by name, citation by citation, from the Victoria Cross and Distinguished Service Order to Conspicuous Gallantry Medal and Distinguished Service Medal, not to mention a host of 'commendations' and 'mentions'.

George's VC immediately followed the warmest citation of them all to Unwin. Of George, it was recorded 'he assisted Commander Unwin at the work of securing the lighters under heavy rifle and Maxim fire. He was wounded in the head but continued his work and twice subsequently attempted to swim from lighter to lighter with a line.'

The mere mention of 'Maxim' in the citation does, however, pose an interesting conundrum for historians. Contemporary observers such as Admiral Keyes and journalist Ellis Ashmead-Bartlett, as well as current commentators like Peter Doyle, have specifically mentioned machine-guns in their past accounts.

However, for an article in *Military History Monthly* to coincide with the centenary of the landings, Peter Hart wrote:

> *The torrent of fire was such that the British have always believed that there were at least two machine-guns, one high to the left and the other in the walls of the castle, but this seems to fly in the face of hard factual Turkish evidence. The Turkish Army had very few machine-guns, and there appears to be no doubt that the entire 26th Regiment had none at all.*
>
> *Perhaps some of the confusion arises from the 37.5mm Nordenfeld guns, which had a high rate of fire and might, indeed, have been thought of as 'old pattern Maxim guns' by some witnesses.*
>
> *Furthermore, their destructive small shells, when coupled with rapid rifle-fire and the overwhelming masking roar of the massed British machine-guns [a dozen Maxims] firing from aboard the River Clyde, may have confused men with little or no time to think either coolly or calmly about what exactly was shooting at them. All they knew was that they were being splattered with bullets.*

Clive Harris also told me that a lot of VC citations were written up to include 'Maxim fire' because it sounded more impressive.

Even Doyle seems now to have ridden back a little on an earlier assertion in his 2011 book, *Gallipoli 1915*, as he explained to me: 'The question of "machine guns" at V beach is a knotty one. I am guided by War Diary entries and additional reports, which make specific claims that there were machine guns and that belts/and or bullet cases were found after the battle was over.

'The location of machine guns was plotted on a map by the Naval cartographers, again after the fact. Lined up against this is the body of evidence, all of it negative, that the Ottomans could not have had such weapons, as they were not well equipped. I think it is still moot. Nevertheless, the question is still argued about, often vehemently.'

Maxims or not, the subsequent, global, outpouring of excitement and adulation following the publication of such an uplifting recitation of bravery contrasted dramatically with the mostly slender, at best, nature of the reports, especially at its outset, that had emanated from the Dardanelles.

On the second day of the landings, for instance, all one could find in *The Times*, was a paragraph detailing *'The British Red Cross and the Order of St John have formed a special committee to deal with Red Cross work in the Near East – the Dardanelles, Egypt, Malta &c being included in that area.'*

The following day, the same newspaper reported baldly an official announcement from the War Office and the Admiralty, beneath the headline 'Landing on the Peninsula' with two sub-heads, 'Joint operations' and 'Stubborn resistance':

> *The general attack on the Dardanelles by the Fleet and the Army resumed yesterday. The disembarkation of the Army, covered by the Fleet, began before sunrise at various points on the Gallipoli Peninsula, and in spite of serious opposition from the enemy in strong entrenchments protected by barbed wire was completely successful. Before nightfall large forces were established on shore.*

In the absence of anything remotely substantial, *The Times* decided to offer instead a short contribution from Walter Leaf, the banker and distinguished Homeric scholar, to give its readers – many of whom presumably didn't know who or what was or were 'the Dardanelles' – some sense of the history and local geography. He wrote:

> *The interior of the peninsula of Gallipoli is little known. It has no attractions for the archaeologist as all the ancient sites in it lie on the shores of the Dardanelles – the tumulus by Seddul-Bahr known as the "Tomb of Protestilaus", Maidos, the ancient Madytus, and the now deserted site of Sestus. The Turkish government has severely*

discouraged any travellers who wished to penetrate inland; and the charts record only so much as is visible from the sea. There is probably no survey of the inland part accessible to the public. It appears to consist of fertile but narrow valleys separated by bare hills with steep sides, but difficult to cross, as they are mostly covered with dense scrub knee-high.

In a strange way, this dry, erudite, summary rather neatly encapsulated, long before retrospect more clearly defined it, both the ancient myth and topographical reality of Gallipoli. For, certainly as far as the former is concerned, Professor Gary Sheffield has noted:

'In a decidedly unglamorous war, Gallipoli provides a splash of colour. It was a dramatic strategic stroke, originating in the imagination of Winston Churchill, which sent soldiers and sailors far from the drab trenches of Flanders to a romantic country – familiar, from the pages of Homer, to the classically educated officers who served there.'

The following day *The Times* reported *'good progress by the Allies ... after a day's hard fighting in difficult country ... thoroughly making good their footing'.* Yet, further down that same report was a sidebar headlined, 'The Turkish version', emanating from an 'official telegram from Constantinople' in which enemy losses were '400 dead'. Propaganda, surely.

A week on, in what was described as Prime Minister Asquith's 'cheerful' statement to the Commons about the landings, he outlined the various beach actions and attendant gallantry to a succession of cheers before admitting 'the losses in these operations were heavy' without, unlike 'The Turkish version', giving any specific figures.

Four days later, on 11 May, in a despatch from Mudros dated 8 May, arrived the fullest and most vivid *Times* account yet, beach by beach, of 'The invasion of Gallipoli' which saved its grimmest paragraphs for V Beach, beginning, portentously, *'we now come to the most terrible of all the landings ...'* as it painted a vivid picture of the *River Clyde* and its human cargo.

The report concluded, however, with some admirable, jingoistic, chest-thumping to leaven, perhaps understandably, the preceding mayhem: *'It has cost us dearly to get astride the Gallipoli Peninsula, but there is no finer tale in our history than that of the deeds which were performed on Sunday, 25 April by the Australian, New Zealand and British troops, supported with equal gallantry by the officers and men of the warships.'*

And as if to underscore this Boys' Own-style summation, it added, presciently: *'Many are the stories of the individual gallantry of officers and men which will probably remain for ever untold, and many a hero who deserves the Victoria Cross now lies beneath the soil.'*

No wonder then that the belated dissemination of de Robeck's own despatch would provoke such a similarly unequivocal response from the print media in general, which would then go on to focus in a quite remarkable and often wildly hyperbolic way on Midshipman George and on his lowly naval rank almost as much as on the young man himself.

On a day when the next most dramatic domestic war reportage was the shelling by a German U-boat of the Cumbria coast – 'Little damage done: Fires started but soon put out: no casualty' (*Daily Telegraph*) – the coverage ranged from the shamelessly parochial to the calculatedly cosmopolitan.

Typically, a number of provincial papers felt they had their own special, almost proprietorial, claim on George, already dubbed 'River Clyde Drewry', by one tabloid. These ranged from the *Hull Daily Mail*'s slightly misleading 'Grimsby young man's great bravery' to 'Forest Gate "Middy": How he won the VC', as proclaimed, more accurately, by the *Essex County Chronicle*.

Even the west managed to chip in as its *Western Evening Herald*, based out of Plymouth, found a unique local angle, headlining, cryptically, 'Midshipman Drewry VC: The Brave Lad's Father thanks Teignmouth Captain'. This must have, at least briefly, bemused its readers until they read about the good Captain Ward and his history with George dating back to their voyages together on the *Indian Empire* when they'd twice circumnavigated the globe.

In a short and succinct telegram, Captain Ward had written to George's father – 'Congratulations on your gallant son winning Victoria Cross – his former Captain, Geo P. Ward'. To which, Thomas replied, revealed the *Evening Herald*, 'Dear Captain Ward – Very many thanks for your telegram congratulating me on the fine conduct of my son. I appreciate your message very much and the kindly feeling that prompted you to send it. I shall send it out to the beyond, and I am sure he will be pleased. You know, Captain Ward, that in the *Indian Empire* you made a sailor of him and built up his character of steadfastness in times of stress, and it is undoubtedly owing to the obedient schooling in seamanship which you gave him that he has done so well.'

The national newspapers also latched on with equal fervour. 'How Merchant Taylors' Boy Won Fame in The Dardanelles' pealed the *Daily Sketch*, setting out its stall in the very first paragraph with: *'No finer story of heroism than that of Midshipman Drewry's exploits in the Dardanelles has been written.'* For its most intimate quote, the *Sketch* had cornered George's 'proud mother', Mary Ann, who offered: 'It's just the thing I expected he would do. He has had a remarkable life for a boy.'

With instead, Thomas as its guide, the *Daily Express* detailed George's various worldwide sailing adventures and occasional mishaps as his father suggested 'there is scarcely a part of the world he has not been to.' As for this latest turn of events?

'In his letters home, he has told me very little of his own doings. The only information I have about the deed for which he was awarded the VC has come from his shipmates and others who saw him swimming with Commander Unwin towards the lighter with a rope between his teeth and amid a hail of shell.

'His last letter, for instance, has very little reference to himself but he is full of praise for Commander Unwin, the other officers and men of the *River Clyde*, and the troops who, he says, were magnificent. I have not seen the boy for two years and I cannot possibly say when he will be coming home. He is still in the Dardanelles.'

Such modesty only helped to fuel the fire of the *Express*'s admiration which, in another prominent corner of that day's paper, blazed even brighter with its 'Matters of Moment' column, subtitled 'Hats Off to the Boy'. This provided a gloriously extravagant, yet oddly patronising commentary on the nature of youthful heroism, which might have come straight out from the pages of the very authors it evoked.

There is no more wonderful and lovable thing on earth than the average British boy. He stands in a class by himself. His morality is his own, based on common sense, and scornful of mere convention. He loathes sentimentality. He is not remarkable for imagination. His literature is his own. He feeds his soul with Marryat, Henty, and Ballantyne, with Stevenson, and sometimes with the elder Dumas, and nowadays with the Kipling of 'The Jungle Book', though rarely with the Kipling of 'Stalky and Co'.

He submits to authority, but invariably apologises to himself for obedience by jeering at all masters behind their backs. He loves soldiers and cricketers and all animals. He is shy and self-conscious with women and foreigners. He hates bullies and 'swank' and everything that is conspicuous and unusual. There is very little difference between the boy at Eton or Marlborough or Tonbridge and the British boy in a well-managed elementary school. The British boy is Peter Pan. There are thousands of him, bearded and grimed, in the Flanders trenches.

The boy has come into his own in Vice-Admiral de Robeck's belated account of the Navy's part in the landing in Gallipoli. Of five VCs, two are given to midshipmen for splendid courage in attempting to secure lighters that had broken loose. These youngsters swam, under heavy rifle and machine-gun fire, from lighter to lighter, carrying lines with them. One was wounded, but he did not stop. They failed, and they tried again. Marryat never conceived a finer deed. D'Artagnan was never braver.

George Drewry and Wilfred Malleson are magnificent young heroes of whom the nation is proud indeed, but they would tell you – and they would be telling nothing but the truth – that they have had the luck, and that hundreds of other fellows would have done just the same if they had the chance. That is a splendid thing to know, and the knowledge makes all the talk of national decadence more than ridiculous. We may thank God for the British boy.'

Yet even as the hearts of *Express* readers must have pounded with pride while they digested this eulogy, it could only begin to paper over the cracks of reality as the numbers of war dead continued to mount up, not least among them a significant proportion of that generation that might be characterised as 'the British boy'.

The *Express* was by no means alone in offering a highly coloured paean to the gallantry at Gallipoli and midshipmen in particular. Without referring directly to George, the *Globe and Traveller*, a venerable evening newspaper, once the oldest in the world, which underscored its emphatic headline, 'Midshipmen Courageous' with the rather more mysterious sub-head, 'Sucking Nelsons', opined as follows:

The midshipman of the British Navy is really a wonderful person. When he goes afloat for the first time, at the age of 16, he is loaded with responsibilities that would bend the back of many a grown man. And before everything else he is taught that danger is a thing to welcome, and that the only unforgiveable crime is cowardice.

The 'snotty' – he still bears the nickname that was bestowed on him by Nelson with those three small brass buttons on his coat-sleeves – is a well-tried man ere he has been at sea for a dogwatch, as sailors have it. He is sent away in charge of his boat on wild nights, with seas that to a landsman would seem sure death to any small craft that was ever launched. He puts off, and he has to see to it that he returns his boat undamaged, his crew uninjured.

They make no song about it, the men of the sea – they simply make the 'snotty' realise what they expect of him. They do not praise, but they blame. They are so keenly jealous of the honour of the Service, that they try the youth very thoroughly ere he is admitted to the sacred fellowship of the ward room ...

And so on and so forth, inevitably echoing, on the way, Marryat and Jack Easy before its stirring Big Finish:

When the lives of several midshipmen were lost in the North Sea tender-hearted people wrote letters to the Press protesting against boys being sent into danger. The whole point of the matter is that 'Snotties' are not boys, but sixteen-year-old mature men. The sea is a hard task mistress and takes one in one's youth to mould as she will.

A naval officer cannot be fashioned after the manner of a subaltern. Knowledge of his duties is the least he has to learn. He must learn the manner of the Navy, and to do that he must be caught young, taken away from the influences of public school and 'Varsity, and taught the Law of the Seven Seas at the end of a tarred rope – metaphorically, but not altogether metaphorically!

It is a system that breeds men – even such men as these boys who have been awarded the highest prize a fighter knows. It is not even that they are consciously brave – it is simply that all these things come in a day's work. It is the 'Navy way'.

While it's tempting to dismiss the *Globe*'s somewhat condescending gush as less an objective outpouring and more as part of some kind of insidious recruitment drive, it must be set against the backdrop of a war that far from being 'over by Christmas' was actually a year into a terrible conflict which now seemed never-ending with good news at a premium. George, for the time being at least, needed to be its poster boy.

A long editorial in *The Nation*, a radical weekly, was altogether more considered as it mused widely if at times a little densely – invoking a *dramatis personae* that bewilderingly spanned Boswell, Johnson, Socrates and the Swedish King Charles XII – on the nature of 'Courage and Civilisation'.

> *'If the good fairy,' it asked, more simply, 'who used to give men "three wishes" were to ask a multitude of healthy males whether they would rather win the VC or die loaded with academic honours, or covered with orders, nine men at least in ten would choose the VC.'*

Referring more directly to the action, it noted, *'The picture lives in the memory of Midshipman Drewry swimming about with a bullet wound in his head, until he had linked up the lighters with a rope.'*

It ends sagely: *'The more civilisation means in the affirmation of human dignity, the more widely it permits to the workers and to women the freedom and the self-respect which were once manly and aristocratic privileges, the more it will develop courage. War may test this virtue, but it cannot make it.'*

Not all the tributes played the simplistic card. *Truth*, a campaigning British periodical, decided instead to mark the occasion by varnishing its appreciation of valour with a very heavy coating of eye-opening candour:

> *Everybody will be glad that a shower of Victoria Crosses has at last descended on the Navy. It is rather a cruel irony of fate that so little chance of personal distinction comes to the men to whom we owe our security at home and our ability to hit the enemy, and who during this war have held the seas for us more securely than they were ever held before against equal dangers.*
>
> *The great adventure at the Dardanelles has given the Navy that chance, in no small measure, and the last list of Victoria Crosses shows how that chance has been taken. But in regard to all these formal distinctions it is as well to bear in mind that for every act of heroism*

honoured there are a hundred that pass unrecorded. In this war our heroes will be numbered by hundreds of thousands, but the limelight can fall on a very few.

Is it too much to hope that the award of Victoria Crosses to two midshipmen will prompt the Admiralty to amend the shabby terms on which all these gallant youngsters are serving? They are doing the work and sharing the dangers of men, as the Dardanelles record shows.

Not a few have died at their posts. It is a disgrace to us that they should draw only schoolboys' pocket-money, and that their parents, who have given them to our service, should have to pay heavily for this privilege. After an outcry on this subject in Truth and other papers many months ago, the Admiralty promised to consider the matter. I suggest that there is now no more time for consideration and that the right thing should be done at once.

The role of the midshipman provoked a rather lighter-hearted, response in a popular political and business magazine, *The Bulletin*. The four-part cartoon unfolds: *'In Nelson's days "middies" were always reckoned "hot stuff" – and in spite of being patronised in certain quarters ("What a pretty uniform!" notes an elderly dear) and satirized in others ("Confounded puppy!" barks a veteran naval officer) the young bloods are playing a fine part in the drama of the Dardanelles'*, with the final scene depicting our young hero getting ugly-looking "Johnny Turk" in an arm-lock.

Punch offered, in rather similar vein: *'In a recent article of the grievances of midshipmen* The Times *mentioned their "cheery enthusiasm". When discussing their treatment by the Admiralty, it is said to be even ruddier.'*

Even the society magazine *Tatler* got in on the act. Under a photograph of 'Three cheerful middies off for a beano' – actually a picnic on Imbros just a few days after George sailed out of Suvla Bay in mid-August – the caption reads:

Comparisons are always odious but perhaps we may be allowed to remark that perhaps of all her gallant sons, Jack Tar has the warmest corner in the heart of the British public; and further, without any consideration, we believe the 'middy' is the most popular unit of that most popular service. Affectionately referred to by his superiors as a 'wart', he has appropriately helped to save the face of the service by his gallantry in the terrible landing on the peninsula ... to every middy in our glorious fleet we wish 'Good luck, God speed, and a safe return.'

The photograph, of three clean-cut young men in naval uniform without a seeming care in the world as they set off for an alfresco spread on the Greek island, has been reproduced endlessly down the years. Shot by the distinguished war photographer Ernest Brooks, an enlistee in the RNVR, who would go on to record the Battle of the Somme, its caption reads left to right, 'George Drewry, Wilfred Malleson, and Greg Russell'.

Except that neither George nor Malleson look remotely like any other photographs of them at that time. It was certainly the case that in some subsequent articles about George, an inset photo of Malleson was used by mistake. The *Daily Mirror*, for instance, which used Malleson's image on both a report of George's award and, three years later a picture caption for his funeral, was asked by a grieving father to issue a correction about the latter. So, two days after the offending caption, the *Mirror* dutifully acknowledged its error – except they wrongly initialled George 'J.A. Drewry'!

The mechanism for George's VC began cranking up unhurriedly late on the night of 26 April in a report from Major General Hunter-Weston to Sir Ian Hamilton in which he praised Unwin and George for having performed 'marvels of work and valour', but while it took just a matter of weeks for *The London Gazette* to announce the campaign's first VCs to army men (Doughty-Wylie and Captain Garth Walford), early notice of any Navy achievement seemed noticeably lacking. So much so that Hunter-Weston 'fearing something had gone amiss with the awards process, submitted his own Victoria Cross recommendations' for Unwin and George.

This Hunter-Weston – who, some might argue, arrives rather too belatedly in my narrative – is, of course, the senior officer who commanded the 29th Division, the overall landing force at Cape Helles. Derided variously as 'Hunter-Bunter' and a 'donkey general', Sir Aylmer Gould Hunter-Weston, with his spectacular moustache, taking into account naval concern about currents, had argued successfully, fatally as it transpired, for a daytime landing.

He had also, wrote Alan Moorehead, made a less-than-helpful proclamation to his division <u>before</u> the battle, saying 'heavy losses by bullets, by shells, by mines and by drowning are to be expected'. He was invalided back to England in July suffering from sunstroke and nervous strain.

Exactly a year later, now promoted to lieutenant general and knighted into the bargain, Hunter-Weston looked on as his divisions suffered the worst casualties on the notorious first day of the Somme.

On the matter of VCs, Hunter-Weston needn't have worried too much for it transpired that Rear Admiral Wemyss had started the process himself within days of the landing, for, as he wrote to his wife on 29 April: 'Thank God, I shall have the pleasure of getting 2 of our officers the VC for acts of gallantry and self-abnegation seldom if ever equalled. There must be many such, but only those 2 have so far come under my action.' By 'those 2' he must surely have been referring to Unwin and Drewry.

In fact, two days before that and just a day after the landing was successfully concluded, Wemyss had confided elsewhere, with an insouciance bordering, some might feel, on insensitivity:

'He [Unwin] with two midshipmen and two seamen performed perfect prodigies of heroism and valour, both in trying to connect the lighters and in saving life. These men seemed to bear charmed lives, for though all around them were being shot like rabbits, they escaped with a few grazes from bullets which did them no harm. One seaman was eventually killed but the others all escaped and are all well and are hard at work.'

On 5 May, in a report from his flagship HMS *Euryalus* to Admiral Sir John de Robeck, he formally set out his own roll-of-honour – 'I wish specially to bring to your notice the extraordinarily gallant conduct of the following Officers and Men at V Beach.'

George was third down a list of eight headed by Unwin ahead of Wemyss's accompanying eulogy.

These officers and men showed the utmost gallantry, and absolute disregard for consequences, and worked indefatigably at securing the lighters, etc, to form the bridge from the River Clyde *to the shore under a murderous fire. Undeterred by the fact that almost every man who was attempting to pass over the bridge was hit, they worked on.*

I have since spoken to more than one Military Officer who was in the collier, and they have assured me that the gallantry and cheerful resource of these Officers and men, in most trying circumstances, were beyond the measure of any language they could use ...

I consider that the conduct of both Officers and men who manned the boats of the attacking force, is beyond praise. These men, without hesitation, repeated the operation of landing the troops a second time, under a fire, which, although diminishing, was by no means negligible, and the losses in killed and wounded sustained in the first attack had no effect in diminishing their zeal and ardour.

I regret that I am unable to pick out any special cases for recommendation, but the fact is that, where all showed so much gallantry and determination, it would be difficult to differentiate. Since no individual cases have been brought to my notice, I can only observe that the general dash and daring are worthy of the very finest traditions of the Navy.

Perhaps the most intimate among the recollections of those fraught, dangerous days, and of George in particular, were those of Carnoustie-born 'Geordie' Samson's, as collated in a serialised version of his travails. These appeared across a couple of weeks in the *Sunday Post*, a Scottish newspaper still in its infancy, which clearly revelled in rallying around this local hero, who'd returned from Gallipoli with, the paper trumpeted, *'thirteen bullets still lodged in his back'*.

The coverage must have severely embarrassed the individual who handed Samson, in civvies at the time, a white feather while the sailor was on his way to be lauded at a local public function.

The most severely injured of the surviving *Hussar* trio was still convalescing in his native Scotland when a telegram from his mother informed him he'd won the VC. Under the headline 'George Samson's Adventures with Midshipman Drewry VC', the article with, one suspects, some substantial 'polish' by a *Post* staffer, weaved a jauntily epic tale blending excitement and peril with a healthy dose of mutual respect, no little modesty – and just possibly some fanciful dialogue.

The River Clyde *had not a very long run to do and when we were approaching our objective I was given orders to accompany that gallant young fellow Midshipman Drewry VC on a small hopper which was now alongside the* River Clyde. *This hopper was chartered for the purpose of towing three flat-decked lighters out in front of the* River Clyde *as she was going ashore and thus making for the soldiers a temporary pier.*

Just at the critical moment something went wrong in the engine room of the hopper. I was in the fo'castle at the time and I was rushing to the little hatchway when I almost collided with Midshipman Drewry.

'What's the matter?' asked Mr Drewry when he saw my state of excitement.

'Oh', I said, 'there's something wrong in the engine room, and I am just going to put it right, sir.'

I was very thankful I possessed a knowledge of machinery for I was able to rectify matters below.

Within a few minutes I rejoined Midshipman Drewry and it was now up to us to get out a gangway. I could see from the very first that this was not going to be a very easy task.

We tried our hardest to accomplish the job but we both saw it was hopeless so my companion suggested he should go for assistance. All this time we were under fire and it was really a marvel we were both not hit.

Scarcely was as this very thought passed from my mind when there was a whizz and I saw that the gallant young midshipman had been struck over the left eye.

He reeled and before I could get the chance to do anything for him he had fallen into the water. Just at this moment the firing increased from the hills ashore. I chanced a look over the side of the ship but I could not see anything of the midshipman.

Notwithstanding all the excitement of the position I could not help feeling a sadness at heart for I had now come to the conclusion that the brave young fellow had paid the great penalty.

Not long after I was somewhat startled to hear one of the officers call out: 'Samson, there's a lighter adrift. Let us have a line.' I looked over the side and was somewhat astonished to see Commander Unwin swimming in the water close to the hopper.

I was quickly at this job and then you can imagine my unbounded astonishment and joy when suddenly I saw the head of Midshipman Drewry appear on the surface of the water. His head was swathed in a bandage but as was his wont he was cheery and smiling.

As I learned afterwards Midshipman Drewry had had a very rough time. After being wounded he found it most difficult to keep afloat in the rough sea and despite this bullets were whizzing about him.

After much difficulty he had managed to reach the **River Clyde** *where his wound had been dressed and very pluckily he had dived in to the water when it was seen that a lighter was adrift.*

It was largely though the plucky work of this young fellow that this important work – making the lighters secure – was carried out.

When this had been done Midshipman Drewry came aboard the hopper and you can imagine we shook hands very heartily after the following conversation had taken place.

'Hello, Samson,' said Mr Drewry. 'I thought you were dead. I never imagined you would have got through it all.'

'Why, sir,' I replied, laughingly, 'it is a most remarkable thing that I thought you were dead.'

'Oh, no,' replied Mr Drewry, 'it's a fact that I had to dodge the bullets when I was in the water but I managed to get back to the River Clyde *all right. One thing is certain, Samson, I never expected to see you again alive.'*

'Why, sir,' I replied humorously, 'I do not think they have got a bullet in Turkey to kill me today. I think they are making it for tomorrow.'

'Well,' said Mr Drewry, 'I must congratulate you. You certainly did the right thing in keeping on deck all the time I went overboard for if you had not done so there would have been no more of George Samson.'

When I first stepped ashore from the hopper, I was with Commander Unwin and Midshipman Drewry. We soon made the mooring secure and troops were quickly hurrying ashore to embeach themselves.

The hail of bullets from those Turkish rifles was beginning to take its terrible toll and I soon found fresh duties to perform – that of carrying the wounded from the shore to the hopper from which they were as soon as it was possible transferred to the River Clyde *after which they were taken to the hospital ship.*

In this work, Commander Unwin and Midshipman Drewry worked most gallantly. Every moment they were risking their lives and really it was nothing short of a miracle that they were not hit.

As long as I live I shall treasure memories of the bravery of these men; they hurried hither and thither giving a hand when needed just as if they were aboard the Hussar *in peace time.*

Bullets were whizzing about our heads every few minutes and we were soon aware of the fact that machine guns were in operation now that our forces were beginning to land in big numbers.

Men were falling down like ninepins quite near us and perhaps it was only the thought that we must give them a helping hand that made us forget our own danger.

I know my officers rendered yeoman service and in several cases wounded soldiers might easily have sustained fatal injuries had they not been properly removed by these heroes.

Among many letters of congratulation to Samson was one from Thomas Drewry who wrote: 'My son has often told me how gallantly you behaved.'

While it is likely that George's parents remained unaware at that time of their son's vicarious fame north of the border, they certainly would have been cheered by a letter they received from Surgeon Peter Burrowes Kelly, which coincided with the onset of the *Post*'s cheerleading for Samson.

In the letter of 3 September, a blend of admiring, spiritual and oddly garbled, Kelly wrote:

'I am taking the liberty now – I meant to take it before but I could not get the address – of writing to you just a few lines about your most gallant of sons, our beloved Midshipman who has made himself and incidentally all those with him famous. I maintain that I am the only person living who can ever know what Commander Unwin and your son did on April 25 both before and after they were knocked out. Why both were not killed I cannot tell you and one must look to someone higher for the reason, God alone can only know – I saw them flushed with victory, faced with defeat and death and so on turn about.

When the Commander lay in a dangerous condition your son took over sole charge, when your son was finished Commander

Unwin was ready although unfit to relieve him. George has a tremendous future in front of him, because his fame will not affect him but only tend to elevate him still higher. His absolute contempt of death, love of duty and modesty were proverbial amongst us all both Military and Naval. You must indeed be proud of this splendid fellow and that he will be spared for many years to gladden your hearts is my one wish.

To have been with such a body of Naval men has been a great honour indeed and I shall never forget that I was their doctor who did what little I could for them all. All were great but *River Clyde* Drewry as he is now known was the greatest. He and Samson have borne out Nelson's old dictum 'My guns may change, my ships may change, but the spirit of my men remains.'

Trusting you will pardon this intrusion on my part and again asking you to accept my warmest congratulations on being the parents of such a man.'

Strange to relate that HMS *Hythe*, a former cross-Channel ferry, from which Kelly had penned this fulsome testimonial, was sunk off Cape Helles, just two months later after colliding with HMS *Sarnia*, an armed boarding steamer, with the loss of 155 lives. Happily, there is no record that Kelly was on board at the time, and the sports-loving Irish–born doctor survived to become Lieutenant Surgeon at the Royal Naval College, Osborne on the Isle of Wight.

Twice wounded, first in his right shin then in his left foot, he received a DSO following this citation from Admiral de Robeck: 'He remained in *River Clyde* until the morning of the 27th, during which time he attended 750 wounded men, although in great pain and unable to walk during the last 24 hours.'

Meanwhile, Samson, five years George's senior, who died of pneumonia in Bermuda in 1923, aged just 34, was the first of the *Hussar* crew to come home and also the first to receive his VC from King George V exactly a month after his newspaper 'splash'. Commander

Unwin's followed in January 1916 then Williams' posthumously on 16 November.

Six days after that, on 22 November, George, now an acting lieutenant, was at Buckingham Palace with members of his family where he was the single VC that day among some fifty Naval and military honours handed out by King George. It was reported that the monarch 'heartily congratulated the recipient and shook hands with him most cordially'.

While George's selfless courage was undeniable, battlefield tour guide Clive Harris offered me another, thought-provoking, angle on the award:

'You could say his VC was as much about life-saving as it was about soldiering. He would have been spurred on by others around him doing the same thing, but it's a collective award. Losing consciousness, regaining it and then getting on with it. The peer pressure from your comrades was unique on 25 April because they were taking a lot of incoming and not putting anything back. By not actively participating in the landing as such, there might have been an element of survivor guilt about his response.'

Ralph, now 18, was the only other brother to see George receive his gong. But if he thought he might get to learn more about the heroic action than had been confided in George's letter home the year before, he'd be disappointed. For, as he told Michael Moynihan more than fifty years later, 'it was about the bravery of others he talked. He said he was only doing his duty and had never expected the VC. When I showed him all the newspaper cuttings about him that we had kept he told me to put them in the toilet.'

Perhaps the most poignant passage in Samson's earlier account was when he declared: '*I do not think I ever felt more satisfied than I did when I heard that Midshipman Drewry had been awarded the VC, especially now that I shall be able to share his company at Buckingham Palace. That very fact will make one proud.*' Sadly, they would never meet again after their V Beach feats.

On 1 December, a little over a week after his visit to the Palace, George travelled to Liverpool for another presentation, of the Sword of Honour, from the Imperial Merchant Service Guild to 'their member Midshipman George Leslie Drewry RNR the first officer of the Royal Naval Reserve and the Merchant Service to win the Victoria Cross'.

At the event, George signed a copy – 'to commemorate a Happy Day' – to the Liverpool's Lord Mayor and Mayoress of artist Norman Wilkinson's beautifully-illustrated Dardanelles memoir which had been published the year before.

Sir Ian Hamilton's first Gallipoli despatch, printed in the third supplement of *The London Gazette* of 6 July offered the Army's first coolly official appraisal of the V Beach landing, though you had to read between the lines to put more flesh on the bones of George and his shipmates' bravery.

Now came the moment for the River Clyde *to pour forth her living freight; but grievous delay was caused here by the difficulty of placing the lighters in position between the ship and the shore. A strong current hindered the work and the enemy's fire was so intense that almost every man engaged upon it was immediately shot. Owing, however, to the splendid gallantry of the naval working party, the lighters were eventually placed in position, and then the disembarkation began.*

A company of the Munster Fusiliers led the way; but, short as was the distance, few of the men ever reached the farther side of the beach through the hail of bullets which poured down upon them from both flanks and the front. As the second company followed, the extemporised pier of lighters gave way in the current. The end nearest to the shore drifted into deep water, and many men who had escaped being shot were drowned by the weight of their equipment in trying to swim from the lighter to the beach. Undaunted workers were still forthcoming, the lighters were again brought into position ...

However, there was absolutely no ambiguity in Sir Ian's concluding comments as he paid fulsome tribute to the Senior Service:

> *Throughout the events I have chronicled the Royal Navy has been father and mother to the Army. Not one of us but realises how much he owes to Vice-Admiral de Robeck; to the warships, French and British; to the destroyers, mine sweepers, picket boats, and to all their dauntless crews, who took no thought of themselves, but risked everything to give their soldier comrades a fair run in at the enemy.*

How ironic that, just a month after this account and even before the various media began busily to extol the Navy for its deeds at the campaign's first amphibious landing in April, so yet another, almost as problematic and potentially disastrous, had been undertaken ahead of this print storm.

But thanks to the strictures of the censors, it would be several more days before news first began to filter through to a nation still consumed with patriotic fervour about the Allied operations at Suvla Bay, of which George would be much more than just an interested observer.

> *A P&O Cadet – the son of Mr Drewry, our Works Superintendent, a boy of 18* [sic] *– has won the VC. (Bravo). His father tells me the boy says he intends to return to the P&O Co when the war is over. Let us hope that he will win through and rise to be Commodore of the P&O Fleet.*

> P&O Chairman Lord Inchcape, addressing shareholders
> at the Annual General Meeting, 8 December 1915

Chapter 6

Suvla Bay: from 10am, 6 August

It should be said that the beaches of Suvla are not the beaches of seaside resorts, all pleasant, smooth sand and shingle. They are called beaches because they cannot well be called cliffs. They slope into the sea with some abruptness, in pentes *of rock and tumbles of sand-dune difficult to land upon from boats. From them one climbs onto sand-dune into a sand-dune land which is like nothing so much as a sea-marsh from which the water has receded. Walking on this soft sand is difficult: it is like walking in feathers; working, hauling and carrying upon it is very difficult. Upon this coast and country, roadless, wharfless, beachless and unimproved, nearly 30,000 men landed in the first ten hours of the 7th of August.*

John Masefield

'We all knew there was going to be a new landing but where and when none knew but the very heads until almost the day it happened,' George wrote in a long letter home dated 28 September.

This was the first – followed by the next in October and the last in November – of three more letters to his father as he embarked on a very detailed personal chronicle of his active involvement in the campaign's second great invasion, a little over three months after the Battle of the Beaches.

'I promised you my account of the Suvla landing and after seeing many photos and accounts in the papers, I think I can tell you my version without offence to the censor,' noted George, in an unconscious reference to what had been effectively a news blackout for almost a fortnight following the start of the operation on 6 August.

Yes, there were sketchy reports of 'New Gallipoli Landings' within a week, which were referred to coyly by Sir Ian Hamilton as only having taken place 'elsewhere'. The first specific mention of Suvla in *The Times* arrived on 19 August in a single column which stated that *'a short advance was made to straighten the line, and under considerable gun and rifle fire the British troops gained some 500 yards, captured a trench, and took a number of prisoners.'*

The following day, the intelligence was fleshed out, albeit disturbingly, headlined 'Heavy losses in Gallipoli. Newly-landed force at a standstill.' A *Times* report five days after that, on 25 August, confirmed *'the recent heavy and costly fighting'* but in a long and fierce editorial salvo aside questioned the true nature of the situation and the veracity of the reportage to date:

No real news comes from the Dardanelles but a steady and swelling stream of casualties. Therefore we are at a loss to understand why the Press Bureau earlier this week permitted the publication of a highly coloured narrative which was at variance with its own authoritative version. It has led the public to believe that the new landing threatens to cut the Turkish communications and in consequence they have even been told that the position of the enemy is critical.

There is nothing in Mr Ashmead-Bartlett's [Ellis Ashmead-Bartlett was the only officially sanctioned London war correspondent in the campaign] *account, or in the Press Bureau's own statement to justify these assumptions. The real conclusion to be drawn is that the position in the Gallipoli Peninsula has so far undergone no material change for the better. We can understand renewed affirmations of our determination to achieve our object at any sacrifice. We do not understand the publication of narratives which cannot in the least deceive the enemy, but which have the unfortunate result of producing among our own public hopes which are no nearer attainment.*

No doubt our censors expressly disclaim responsibility for the accuracy of reports submitted to them. But why is it that the general

The four Drewry brothers in 1901; l-r: Percy (11), Harry (13), Ralph (4) and George (7). (*Heather Thorne*)

Drewry family photo; 1908 l–r: Harry, George, Thomas, Mary Ann, Ralph and Percy. (*Heather Thorne*)

George (right), 14, with oldest brother, Harry. (*Heather Thorne*)

No.53 Kitchener (formerly Haslemere) Road, Forest Gate. (*Quentin Falk*)

No.58 Claremont Road, Forest Gate. (*Quentin Falk*)

The ships of George Drewry:
SV *Indian Empire*; SS *Isis* (P&O
Heritage Collection); HMS *Hussar*
(Imperial War Museum); HMS
Conqueror (MOD, Naval Historical
Branch); HMT *William* Jackson (after
being renamed SV *Evelyn Rose*).
(*Bernard McCall*)

H.M.S. CONQUEROR.

The *River Clyde*
approaching V Beach.
(*Stephen Chambers*)

V Beach, today and inset, April 1915.
(*Quentin Falk / Imperial War Museum*)

George (head bandaged) with Dr Peter
Burrowes Kelly after V Beach landing.
(*Central News*)

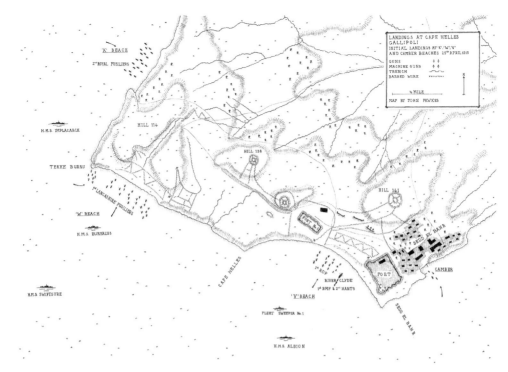

Map of Cape Helles. (*John Fawkes*)

Map of Suvla Bay. (*John Fawkes*)

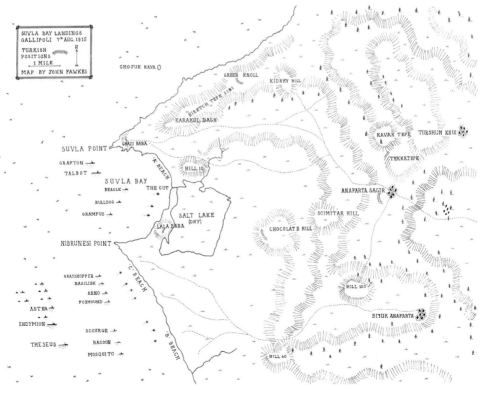

South-looking view of A Beach, Suvla Bay, 2018 (Quentin Falk)/Landing at A Beach, August 1915. (*Norman Wilkinson*)

Three 'middies' on Imbros, August 1915. Officially captioned, l–r: George, Wilfred Malleson, Greg Russell. More likely – Russell, Malleson and Drewry. (*Imperial War Museum*)

Among the crew, with HMS *Hussar* officers, autumn 1916: top row, l-r: Hewetson, Moore, Burton, Ellis; middle row, l-r: Giffard, Heneage, Hennessey; front row, l-r: George, Simeon, Fletcher. (*Heather Thorne*)

George (right) off duty with fellow officers on Imbros. (*Imperial War Museum*)

At the palace for his investiture, November 1916: l–r, Ralph (left) and George with their mother Mary Ann. (*Imperial War Museum*)

Daily Sketch front page, 22 November 1916. (*John Frost Newspapers / Alamy Stock Photo*)

Scapa Flow 2018 and, inset, during the Great War. (*Angus Konstam / Orkney Library and Archive*)

Portrait of a VC. (*Heather Thorne*)

THE V.C. MIDDIES OF THE DARDANELLES.

Midshipman George L. Drewry, R.N.R., winning the Victoria Cross by swimming from lighter to lighter with a rope during a heavy fire from rifles and maxims. On the left of the picture is seen the "River Clyde," from which the troops were landed. Inset are portraits of Midshipman G. L. Drewry, V.C., R.N.R. (left), and Midshipman W. St. A. Malleson, V.C., R.N. (right).

(*Drawn for the "Boy's Own Paper" by* ALGERNON BLACK.)

'The VC Middies of the Dardanelles'. (*Boy's Own Paper*)

George (foreground) with bandaged head during his VC action as featured in *Deeds that Thrilled an Empire: Vol 1*). (*N&M Press*)

Cartoon from *The Bulletin*, 18 August 1915. (*Heather Thorne*)

Front and back cover of *The Hornet*, 5 November 1966. (*DC Thomson & Co Ltd*)

Detail of the hopper *Argyle* in the 1938 diorama of the V Beach landing. (*Imperial War Museum*)

Centenary commemorative stone to George in Central Park, East Ham. (*Richard Tedham*)

George T. Drewry, George's oldest surviving nephew. (*Quentin Falk*)

The author at Suvla Bay. (*John Mackenzie*)

effect of their handiwork is to express the disagreeable truth and to pass the cheerful falsehoods?

George's own Suvla story began three weeks earlier in Mudros at the end of July shortly before he'd learn about the announcement of his VC. He had recovered from his wounds after V Beach and rejoined HMS *Hussar* as the ship resumed her gunboat and minesweeping duties.

Ahead of the new August initiative, *Hussar*'s most significant action took place towards the end of June some 250 miles south of Canakkale when, off the island of Chios, it bombarded three Ottoman ports, Tehesme, Lidia and Aglelia [now Cesme, Ildir and Alacati] – all seaward of the great ancient Anatolian city of Smyrna which itself had been severely attacked by the Navy in March – destroying several sailing craft and a petroleum depot.

Having dreamed up the 'Wooden Horse' gambit and consolidated it with his own persistence and fortitude, Unwin was the obvious choice to be at the vanguard of any new amphibious assault on the peninsula.

The offensive at Suvla Bay, 20 miles and 3 miles, respectively, north of Cape Helles and Anzac Cove, was intended by Hamilton as a complementary operation, on beaches designated A, B and C, to heavily-armed attacks at those other two principal sectors. Unwin was given the job of supervising troop-, horse- and mule-laden X-lighters (motor-landing craft, known as 'Black Beetles') which had been initially towed to Mudros all the way from Devonport, beginning back in June.

Each capable of holding 400 fully-equipped men, they were constructed of bullet-proof iron, drew 4½ feet of water, and in the bows of each was a solid gangboard (or 'brow') capable of being lowered to the beach so enabling the troops to reach the shore with dry feet. The lighters were given an operational 'K' number. They would also protect the men much more effectively than the open boats used in the 25 April landings.

With the campaign effectively stalemated on the peninsula, Hamilton's by now severely depleted force was finally augmented by three of Kitchener's volunteer 'New Army' divisions for what Peter Doyle described as an 'all or nothing moment' in the faltering offensive.

On 31 July George met up with Unwin in the harbour at Lemnos and asked him if he required a 'snottie' at his side: 'He said he had no job for me but promised to take me up to the landing if I could get permission. He worked it alright and on the 2nd or 3rd of August I put a shirt or two in a pillow case and joined up on K-14, that being Unwin's flagship.'

George then explained to his father that 'K-14 was similar to the other lighters except that she was fitted for a 4.7in [gun] which,' he then added, mysteriously, 'was at the bottom of some supply ship's hold and not to be got at.'

For his part, in early May, Unwin had left *Hussar* and been posted to Egypt before assuming command of the cruiser HMS *Endymion*. After sailing her to Mudros, he then took up his crucial new role in charge of all motor lighters for a planned second landing on the peninsula.

At 10am on 6 August, George and his fellow officers were told 'today's the day', and to arrange themselves 'brow down on the quay and wait'.

'Then we began to think it would be put off as the wind began to rise from the SW just where we did not want it. However, it died early in the afternoon and conditions became ideal. At 3pm we were told what to do but even then we were not told exactly where we were landing but simply run in where we were slipped by our towing vessel.

'At 4pm we started to embark soldiers from the beach to the towing vessels, and I tell you, Dad, it was a most glorious sight,' he enthused, in exactly the same fashion as his excited declaration three months earlier en route to Cape Helles.

'Imagine a fleet of fourteen or so motor lighters darting backward and forward between the beach and ships, those going looking [like] a blot of karki [*sic*], the beach a mass of soldiers. Besides the lighters were tugs and trawlers towing horse boats and barges. What a panic would have taken place if Fritz had flown over with a few bombs.'

It all went off, wrote George, 'without a hitch. At dark we sailed, surely the strangest fleet that has ever sailed. First came the towing ship full of troops, then the lighters with 600, and astern of her was the picket boat attached to her (each lighter had one).'

For George, it might at this stage have all seemed to be going without a hitch, but ensconced at his headquarters on Imbros, Hamilton's eve-of-invasion concerns were obvious as revealed in his diary entry for that day, which began with a quote from an early eighteenth century hymn:

'O! God of Bethel, by whose hand thy people still are fed, I am wishing the very rare wish, that it was the day after tomorrow. Men or mice we will be by then, but I'd like to know which. K's New Army, too! How will they do? What do they think? They speak – and with justice – of the spirit of the Commander colouring the morale of his men, but I have hardly seen them, much less taken their measure. One more week and we would have known something at first hand.'

Meanwhile, George continued his less emotional narrative: 'Unwin had a picket boat to himself and this one towed astern of another picket boat towing astern of a motor lighter which was towing astern of a ship. Midshipman Price RN DSC was running the picket boat, I was simply a passenger.'

Midshipman James Charles Woolmer Price was a survivor from HMS *Ocean*, which had struck a mine and sunk in March at Morto Bay.

As this so-called 'strange' flotilla sailed for shore, there was supporting fire from Cape Helles and from flanking ships, making, noted George, 'a jolly fine display. Then as we approached Anzac a searchlight opened up just past the hospital ships onto the Anzac hills', followed by 'immense bombardment' of the still distant shore.

'It was a remarkable sight from the sea. One large space of hillside lit up brilliantly by the destroyer searchlights and exploding shells and star lights; at sea nothing to be seen except the numerous hospital ships anchored off Anzac with their band of red and green lights; and yet the sea teemed with life.'

Around 11.30pm, the various boats stopped and all cast off their tows by then being close in to shore even though only the outline of the beach could be made out. 'Of course,' continued George, 'silence and no lights was the order but the motors seemed to make a terrible row and I think everyone cursed them under their breath.'

At this moment, some grisly memories of the V Beach disembarkation came flooding back for George as well as for many of the others. 'It was not a happy sensation for we all remembered the last landing and what we met, what was going to happen if they expected us, they would mow us down, for our decks were thick with soldiers.

'But,' he explained, 'they were expecting us in another place and we got ashore practically without casualties,' thus confirming at least some positive aspect of Hamilton's grand plan which, at its most simplistic, comprised a three-pronged assault along the peninsula from different locations under conditions of extreme secrecy with, hopefully, some chance of 'hoodwinking' (as Hamilton optimistically described it) the Turks.

'A slight description of the country in which this attempt to straddle the peninsula was taking place may be of interest, as seen from the sea,' wrote the artist Norman Wilkinson RNVR. 'On our left Suvla Point, with Nibrunesi Point to our right, formed a small bay known as Suvla Bay some mile and a half across. On the right of Nibrunesi Point a long gently curving sandy beach some four or five miles in extent terminated where the Australian position at Anzac rose steeply to the Sari Bair range. Inside and immediately in front of us was a large flat sandy plain covered with scrub, while the dry salt lake showed dazzlingly in the hot morning sun.

'Immediately beyond was Chocolate Hill, and behind this again lay the village of Anafarta, some four miles from the shore. As a background, the Anafarta range ran from the village practically parallel with the sea until it took a sharp turn due west to Suvla Point, where it gradually sloped down to the coast. Beyond the plain in front of us a number of stunted oaks, gradually becoming more dense further inland, formed excellent cover for the enemy's snipers – a mode of warfare at which the Turk has become an adept.'

C Beach – 'beautiful ... with a good stretch of clean white sand and then a ridge with scrub over which we could not see without going up to it' – where George first landed, was, like B beach next to it, a mile or so below Nibrunesi Point, which marked the southern tip of the crescent-shaped bay.

At C Beach, 'the lighters were able to beach just where we wanted ... and when the brow was towed the men were able to walk ashore with dry feet.'

It was, however, a rather different story at A Beach in the heart of the bay itself, as George described it: 'Unfortunately [it] was not a great success, as the water was very shallow and men had to wade ashore some distance up to their waist.

'Most casualties were here. They met a party of about 50 almost at once [but] a short fight soon dispersed them. They landed a little earlier there than us at C & B and the firing sounded very funny as it started just as we landed. Then here and there along the coast a rifle would go off and a few bullets flew around but I saw nobody hit. When we cast off from our tow we stopped for a few minutes long enough for the first lighter to reach the beach and then ran in and saw she was all right. We visited them all as they ran ashore and saw things were going well.'

Apart, that is, from one lighter which seemed to have gone missing altogether, so, knowing her number, George together with Unwin went in search of her towards Nibrunesi Point. 'We soon found her astern of her tow with her engine seized. *Glory*'s steamboat was attached to her so we told *Glory* to make fast alongside port and we made fast on starboard, and like that we ran her ashore quite successfully. Then

Unwin went off to bring the motor engineer and left me to see things went right.'

HMS *Glory* was a Royal Navy battleship of the Canopus class.

George continued: 'I stayed on various lighters until ashore and had a run on the beach but it was uncanny, the troops got ashore in record time and then came batteries and mules and munitions. I could not understand it, I stood on the beach and saw guns being landed and horses and behind us a few yards was dark bush, containing what?

'There was little firing, now and then a sharp rattle quite close, and then silence. I thought of Helles and wondered … if we were ambushed … the Maxims were … going to clear the beach of living in one sweep.

'Then a thing happened that was bad for nerves. A motor suddenly caught fire and lit the whole beach up for about five minutes and then went out, doing no damage to itself. At daybreak they started to shell us but not very heavily … light, nasty things that make a horrible hissing noise.'

So as we leave George just after sunrise on 7 August, what was the much bigger military picture beyond his own intimately vivid recollection of those first few hours of action?

According to Hamilton, with the combination of 'a vigorous offensive from Anzac, combined with a surprise landing to the north of it, I meant to try and win through to Maidos, leaving behind me a well-protected line of communications starting from the bay of Suvla.'

Maidos was an Ottoman stronghold on the peninsula, now called Eceabat, almost directly opposite Canakkale.

The three-pronged attack was initially launched from Mitylene (Mytilini on Lesbos), Lemnos – in George's case – and Imbros, respectively 120, 60 and 15 miles out from Gallipoli under conditions of such secrecy – 'much too much so as it turned out', Unwin wrote later – that, for instance, even the commander of the Mitylene force had no idea of his destination or what he was intended to do until informed by the captain of the ship in which he was conveyed to the scene.

Commanding the Suvla sector and IX Corps was 61-year-old Lieutenant General the Hon Sir Frederick Stopford, like so many of the other ageing Army chiefs in the day, a veteran of the Sudan and the Boer War. He was, as caustically described in his memoir by John Hargrave of the Royal Army Medical Corps, 'one of those stubborn, mulish men, with a big egg-shaped head that dwindled downwards into inconclusiveness. The tired, burnt-out eyes stared down a melancholy flutelike nose from which depended an obstinate upper lip bushed with a pepper-and-salt moustache. Every feature said, "No, I'm not going to! – not yet anyhow ..."'

Aboard de Robeck's flagship, the sloop HMS *Jonquil*, for the fifty-minute crossing from Imbros to Suvla, Stopford spent most of the time spelling out his concerns regarding the whole enterprise to the admiral; principally that he didn't have sufficient ordnance to dislodge an entrenched enemy.

While, as George had correctly noted, the landings on B and C Beaches went near perfectly, his on A Beach was 'not a great success' which was to prove something of an understatement.

According to Hamilton: 'The landing at A was more difficult, both because of the shoal water and because there the Turkish pickets and sentries – the normal guardians of the coast – were on the alert and active. Some of the lighters grounded a good way from the shore, and men had to struggle towards the beach in as much as 4ft 6in of water. Ropes in several instances were carried from the lighters to the shore to help to sustain the heavily accoutred infantry.

'To add to the difficulties of 34 Brigade, the lighters came under flanking rifle fire from the Turkish outposts at Lala Baba and Ghazi Baba. The enemy, knowing every inch of the ground, even crept down in the very dark night on to the beach itself, mingling with our troops and getting between our firing line and its supports. Fortunately the number of these enterprising foes was but few, and an end was soon put to their activity on the actual beaches by the sudden storming of Lala Baba from the south.'

Lala Baba was a 160ft high hill between Nibrunesi Point and a dry salt lake.

That official version, which only became public record the following January, seems, like George's, similarly restrained, certainly compared with more contemporary re-evaluations. Among others, Peter Hart, describes that landing as a disaster, using eye-witness accounts to paint a picture of heavily-laden men having to disembark well short of the beach in waters varying in depth between 5ft and 12ft before coming under fire.

One of those accounts came from Captain Geoffrey Meugens of the 11th Manchester Regiment, which not only contradicted some of Hamilton's version but also, by extraordinary coincidence, added a little more detail to the otherwise sketchy last hours of my wife's great uncle, Major Jack Sillery, whose fate had drawn me to Gallipoli in the first place.

Of the chaos and confusion as lighters stuck on sandbanks became easy targets, Captain Meugens explained: 'As a final expedient the men were pushed and packed back to the stern to take the weight off the bows and so get off the obstruction, but this proved futile. Finally, it was decided for a few men to go over the end with a rope attached to the lighter and take this ashore [*shades of V Beach*] and that the remainder should get to shore as best they could hanging on to the rope and pulling themselves along by it.

'The CO called for tall men and I being about 5ft 11ins stepped forward. Our Second in Command, Major Sillery, was going over first. He turned to me and said, "I advise you to take off all your equipment like me." I did so and jumped in after him. I went clean under and could not touch bottom. However, I struck out and in about 5 yards I found my depth. The CO of the 9th Lancashire Fusiliers followed and when we three got to the shore Major Sillery, the Colonel and I hung on to the rope and kept it as taut as we could.'

Is it possible, one is tempted to speculate, that before his untimely death sometime on 7 August, Major Jack Sillery and George might have passed close by each other at Suvla like proverbial, one might even hazard like literal, 'ships in the night'?

> *The morning sun was up as we lay in Suvla Bay ... It lit the famous battlefield ... We would have been dull fools if we had gazed otherwise than spellbound at this sunlit landscape, where the blood of lost battles was scarcely dry upon the ground. What surprised us most was the invisibility of the warring armies ... It was not till noon that a lighter came alongside, and having taken us all aboard, proceeded to make for the beach. All the while the Turk left us unmolested, causing us to wonder whether he were short of ammunition, or just rudely indifferent to our coming to Suvla or our staying away. Two shells or three, we thought, would have had their courteous aspect. But without greeting of any kind from the enemy our lighter rose on the last wave and bumped against the jetty. We gathered our equipment, and with egotistical thrills stepped upon the Gallipoli Peninsula. For the first time we stood in Turkey. We felt in our breasts the pride of the invader.*
>
> Ernest Raymond

Chapter 7

Suvla Bay, from 6am, 7 August – 2am, 9 August

How the lightermen and beetle-masters feared and hated the shallow waters of that lovely bay! Again and again during the hours of semi-darkness the heavy-laden, flat-bottomed barges fouled the sandbanks that lay submerged in three feet of water 200 yards from the shore. And now that the blazing dawn had burst upon us all in all its roseate-golden swordplay, the Turkish gunners in the hills could see the boatloads coming ashore like water-beetles on a stagnant pond. Grounded in darkness on those treacherous shoals, the lighters and landing-beetles were now under shell-fire in the brilliant early morning sunshine.

John Hargrave, *The Suvla Bay Landing*

About an hour after sunrise, George joined Commander Unwin again in the picket boat. They headed north around Nibrunesi Point and into Suvla Bay where, wrote George, with familiar understatement, 'we saw not a cheerful sight'. It seemed that amid all the other bedlam, three of the 'Beetles' were stuck aground and simply couldn't budge. They were also coming under serious fire.

'They were having a fearful time from shell, but, luckily, mostly shrapnel. The [A] beach was getting an awful time. We went on to the flagship (many ships had arrived by this time and anchored south of Suvla Point) and went aboard. It was not a nice morning, breezy and cold, and I was in whites.'

With Nibrunesi Point, Lala Baba hill as well as B and C Beaches 'getting horribly strafed', George was given orders verbally by HMS *Jonquil*'s commander, Rear Admiral Charles Arbuthnot Christian, to round up any available 'Beetles' in order to take troops from the ships to C Beach. On his way back, 'a nasty aeroplane dropped a bomb ahead of us and another one astern. Some excitement,' George noted, phlegmatically.

By the time George returned to the flagship, Unwin was absent on other more urgent business, so he had a little time to take stock and get a clear, if now disturbing, bird's eye view of Suvla as well as a 'good idea of the line. Several tugs were trying to get to the motors that were aground but the fire was too hot and they stayed aground all day.'

Admiral Keyes recalled later how he went aboard two of the stranded lighters and 'found one deserted except for an elderly pensioner torpedo coxswain who was very sober but full of rum. He told us very contemptuously that his officers – a temporary RNR Lieutenant and Midshipman – and the crew had deserted in the lighter's boat when she came under shrapnel fire at daylight. For his part he had stayed "to soothe the dying moments of the wounded".'

In his letter to Lord Wester-Wemyss some years on, Unwin took up that same story from the point when he heard that the same coxswain was to be recommended for promotion to warrant officer for 'his gallant behaviour'. Unwin asked to be allowed to investigate the case first and found the reason for his heroism was that he was in charge of the rum and physically unable to leave it and the lighter!

Around 9.30am, George joined up again with Unwin in the picket boat and they suddenly encountered a 'Beetle' full of ammunition and stores anchored off the shore with, apparently, nobody aboard. George took charge, weighed anchor and headed into B Beach although, to confuse things further, B was now, according to George, 'a wash-out and called C Beach instead'.

To make matters even more hairy, it was being shelled heavily so George headed off into what he reckoned was a quieter anchorage. But as soon as the brow was down, he quickly realized they had run into a makeshift hospital station so had to swiftly back out and anchor a little further up the beach.

'A large working party from *Prince George* soon had the gear going ashore but they shelled us so heavily that they had to knock off several times. It sounded like a hailstorm on our deck and sides but being shrapnel, it did no harm.' The beach party, however, suffered badly, with at least six killed to George's knowledge.

He wrote, 'We were jolly glad to get away from that place and went back to the flagship for orders.' These were to take troops to A Beach. This was, however, a newly-designated A Beach about 400 yards inside Suvla Point, the other one having now been abandoned.

George and Unwin next closed in on one of the ships and filled up with soldiers.

It turned out the beach was more akin to a narrow cove with 'just room for three lighters and I had to wait about twenty minutes. As I went in, Unwin boarded me, cursing the other people for not going in hard enough, and getting their brows dry on the beach.'

Unwin, it seems, now decided to demonstrate just what he required. 'We went in at a fine speed,' George reported, 'and certainly got our brow dry. However, when we wanted to back out, we found we would not budge.

'To make matters worse, another lighter barged into our quarter and sent us up another three feet. A trawler hooked on but could not manage it, so we remained on the beach all night and until 11am the next day. It was rather interesting as I saw two snipers rounded up and some land mines, which were very poor things and did little damage.'

Having been, to all intents and purposes, stranded for several hours on what was officially now called A West Beach, George watched as a trawler tried to 'pluck us off ... but was too unhandy. Then a large paddle tug did the trick easily.'

Then, George complained, started 'the usual round that sickened me. First to the *Jonquil* for orders ... to go to the *Dundrennan* and load. Just made fast to her when three stripes comes up and orders me to *Minneapolis*. Arrive there and Unwin tells me to go to the *Ramargan* [*Ramazan*]. On the way to her I was twice told to go to other ships by various stripes, if I had obeyed everyone I should have kept up a grand tour of Suvla and done no work but salute stripes.'

As far as George was concerned, Unwin's stripes superseded all others, so he headed for the *Ramazan* where after arriving at about 4pm, loaded up with 'forty mules and baggage and about twenty natives all for Anzac', before setting out for the by-now legendary cove with its shallow beach, which would take him about an hour.

The 'natives' in question – George's regular companions over the next few days – were the often gallant drivers of the Indian Mule Corps, which had arrived from France on the first day of the campaign. There were four detachments in all comprising some 2,600 men, more than 4,300 mules and 2,000 carts, each pulled by two mules, not to mention 10,000 tons of hay, barley and maize which had originally accompanied them from India. The main corps was then divided into four Mule Cart Corps on the peninsula.

Because of the nature of the terrain, which was quite unsuitable for motor transport and four-wheeled vehicles pulled by horses, the Mule Cart Corps was not just vital for delivering ammunition and supplies to the front line trenches but also as vulnerable as the troops they were serving. On a particularly dangerous stretch of ground above Anzac which became known as 'Mule Gully' 177 men and 858 mules of the Cart Corps were killed or wounded.

In Richard van Emden and Stephen Chambers' account of Gallipoli 'in Soldiers' Words', Petty Officer David Fyffe of No.3 Armoured Car Squadron, RNAS, offers a rather less than charitable view of at least the quadruped element of the otherwise invaluable Corps: 'A mule is the biggest hypocrite in the animal kingdom. From a front view he will wear a look of the most absolute innocence, a very cherub of a mule, but get anywhere near his stern end and, like a bolt out of the clear sky, will come the most ferocious kick that ever destroyed a man's belief in animal morality.'

So George headed for Anzac, where the legend of the Australian and New Zealand troops had been first forged in April: 'I knew the place only by reputation but found the beach alright and ran into it about half a cable [90 metres] south of Ari Burnu, which is, I believe, "Gurkha Bluff".'

In fact, George believed wrong, for 'Gurkha Bluff' was considerably south of the headland of Ari Burnu, above the old Y Beach of 25 April landings fame. The entrenched promontory had been nicknamed following its successful storming three months earlier, with relatively minor casualties, by Gurkha troops on 12/13 May during the second battle of Krithia.

'Contrary to expectations,' records George, 'no shells hit us, but the rifle firing was very hot and came very close. The mules were out and the natives started on the baggage just as a beach Lieut came along and asked if we were coming again.'

When George nodded, the officer replied, tersely, '"Well, I don't advise you to, it's very unhealthy", or words to that effect. The beach certainly did look unhealthy, almost choked with sunken lighters and boats a little offshore and towards Hell Spit [*the Southern point of Anzac Cove*] … the masts and funnel showing above water. The beach was deserted except for our natives; at the foot of the cliffs were piles of stores and the cliffs themselves were like rabbit warrens.'

It became distinctly more unhealthy just minutes later when there erupted a series of explosions starting at Hell Spit and working their way along the beach towards George and his vessel. One fell just short, but shrapnel splinters dropped on board. The big bangs continued on as far as Ari Burnu, and then ranged all the way back again.

Suddenly 'remembering my Hindustani', George urged his 'natives' on. 'When we were empty we hoisted the brow (done by tackles down below) and went astern but she wouldn't come off and I had to seek the aid of a picket boat.'

The picket boats were attached to buoys out of range and it took fully a quarter of an hour for one to arrive and pull George's lighter clear. Enemy fire followed them out to sea for over a mile but with poor accuracy, thankfully. However, noted George, 'our shelter of 3/8in steel seemed very thin when H.F [*harassing fire*] was flying about.'

He arrived alongside the *Ramazan* at 5pm before shoving off an hour later on what began, he described wittily, as 'a most interesting run past all the freaks of Fred Karno's Navy blazing away on Anafarta'. These were the well-defended hills beyond the Suvla coastline and plain.

They ran into a cove just north of Ari Burnu which proved comparatively tranquil, but couldn't get the brow down so their cargo of horses had to wade ashore in about 4ft of water. A store lighter, K-9, had already arrived and was beam on, unable to come off. While there was no actual shelling at the time, a few stray bullets still pinged in from their left. After unloading, George arranged for a line to K-9 and tried to tow her off, which they managed to do, bow out to sea.

'Just as we were patting our backs on a fine piece of work, our stern touched a bank and we went beam on. After a lot of pushing seaward we pushed her shoreward and came off like a duck. K-9 asked if I was going to have another try but I said I would report him badly aground when I got back to Suvla.'

It was now 8.15pm and George made a good run into Suvla, where after more than two hours of loading, he set off again with a full load of cargo and also towing a horseboat.

'Running at night was rather a panicky experience as we had not joined up Anzac and Suvla and the old motor was rather gaspy. A breakdown and we would have made the acquaintance of "Mr Turko". Also the fleet's nerves are not too good owing to the new ships from the North Sea and we passed several on our way, all darkened, of course.'

Anzac was darkened, too, but George ran in very carefully, using light from the hospital ships.

'Now, Anzac,' explained George, 'is not nice during day but it's awful at night. About half a mile out, feeling our way in, bullets began to hit us and became thick as we got closer, ones from the trenches, almost spent, that make a nasty sighing sound as they come. There was only the cox'n and myself on deck and I had to go right forward to see where we were going. I had no cover and felt most funky.'

Despite this heavy enemy fire, George managed to 'hit the right spot, brow dry and starboard side alongside a pier. Sheer luck as there were few stretches clear of wreckage. Then someone on the pier sang out, "Who the devil are you?" and I recognized Goodbun's voice, *Indian Empire* Goodbun.' It was – 'like one of those meetings you read about in books' – none other than one of George's old shipmates from his three-master globe-trotting 'prentice days.

'*Indian Empire* Goodbun' was Sub Lieutenant Alfred Miller Goodbun RNR, who first arrived in the Eastern Mediterranean in February 1915, aboard the battlecruiser HMS *Inflexible*, which had become the flagship of the Mediterranean fleet a month before. In June, he transferred to the cruiser HMS *Europa*, based at Mudros initially on boom defence duties. His service record indicates that just days after meeting George, his age contemporary, he was appointed lieutenant (temporary). Four years later, in January 1919, he is recorded, less gloriously, as having been admitted to Chatham Hospital suffering from gonorrhea.

The beach itself was, it seems, marginally less dangerous than the shore, with 'only a few bullets falling here and there'. Yet, as George noted, 'the beach party at Anzac are fatalists. They are sure to be killed or wounded. Everyone has so far except Goodbun,' before adding, a little cryptically, 'and he has been scratched twice.'

At this unearthly hour, George was invited to his old chum's dug-out halfway up the cliff. There they had a beer together, reminisced about the past and compared notes on their latest, rather more hazardous, shared experience.

George's indefatigable exploits during his first two days in and around Suvla contrast starkly with the creeping inertia, which had already, almost insidiously, started to overtake official operations at the sector. It rose to a crescendo, as expressed by Captain Arthur Crookenden of 159 Brigade, 53rd Division, among many others.

According to van Emden and Chambers, Captain Crookenden complains bitterly: 'No one at Suvla seemed to care a solitary damn. One's first day of action, terribly keen to get the best out of the Terriers, one had been training, ready and anxious to prove their mettle, confident that they had been well taught, keyed up to a concert pitch, one was absolutely amazed, baffled and finally enraged by this sort of tepid "Fanny Annie" which hit one at every turn. It spread to the ranks like a fog and very rapidly. Nothing can convey the atmosphere of indifference, laissez-faire and chaos into which we plunged.'

John Masefield described the offensive as 'perhaps the strangest and most difficult battle ever planned by a mortal General. It was to be a triple battle, fought by three separated armies, not in direct communication with each other.'

But all these difficulties were 'as nothing to the difficulty of making sure that the men fighting in the blinding heat of a Gallipoli August should have enough water to drink'.

Hamilton later admitted that the 'new troops suffered much from want of water' and that its means of distribution 'proved to be inadequate and that suffering and disorganization ensued'.

Best known for novels like *Sinister Street*, *Monarch of the Glen* and *Whisky Galore*, Compton Mackenzie, commissioned in the Royal Marines but seconded to Intelligence in the campaign, recalled the day very bleakly in his 1929 memoir, *Gallipoli Memories*: 'It was a long time before I fell sound asleep, for I kept waking to clutch at phantoms. There was no vestige of hope left in my mind that the Suvla landing could now succeed. I felt as if I had watched a system crash to pieces before my eyes, as if I had stood by the deathbed of an old order. The guns I could hear might have been a growling that foretold the murderous folly of the Somme. The war would last now until we had all turned ourselves into Germans to win it. An absurd phrase went singing through my head. "We have lost our amateur status tonight."'

General Stopford had been languishing in semi-retirement as Lieutenant of the Tower of London until plucked for Dardanelles duty

– principally because Hamilton's first picks for command were already preoccupied on the Western Front and, more specifically, blocked by Lord Kitchener. He directed, if that's the right word, the operations from on board HMS *Jonquil* though it was rumoured he had slept soundly through the actual landing itself.

Although the plan was initially to secure the bay as a safe harbour and base for future operations, it was also felt that if the new divisions acted quickly enough after landing they could outflank the Turks occupying the nearby hills. Whether it was directly a result of Stopford's own 'escalating caution' – as noted by Peter Hart – or the influence exerted over the general by his divisional commanders who believed themselves unable to move their troops due to a combination of exhaustion and thirst, the result was a period of fatal inaction.

Nine days after the landing, General Stopford was dismissed, only to be replaced by General Julian 'Bungo' Byng who had, ironically, topped Hamilton's list for command in the first place.

For George, immune from the vagaries of high command and military in-fighting, it was now 2am on 9 August.

By climbing into the foretop of the vessel, it was possible to watch the living cinema of battle. Glasses were necessary to distinguish the light khaki of our men against the scrub and sand. The troops marching in open order across the salt lake formed a most stirring picture as they crossed the unbroken surface of silver-white. Overhead shrapnel burst unceasingly, leaving small crumpled forms on the ground, one or more of which would slowly rise and walk shorewards while others lay where they fell. Beyond this open space it became almost impossible to follow the movements of the battle, but the continual rattle of musketry showed where the advance was proceeding into the more thickly wooded plain. Our hopes that the surrounding ridges would be taken before nightfall were unfortunately not realized.

Norman Wilkinson

Chapter 8

Suvla Bay: From 2am, 9 August – 1.30pm, 12 August

At Suvla when a sickening curse of sound
Came hurtling from the shrapnel-shaken skies
Without a word you shuddered to the ground
And with a gesture hid your darkening eyes.

Geoffrey Dearmer

Following the briefest of encounters at Anzac, including the swiftest of ales with his old pal Goodbun, George shoved off for Suvla after also making sure all the mules were properly unloaded on to the beach.

However, he was almost immediately confronted with more problems: 'The lighters would not back straight astern but slewed round at once, so for the first half mile or so you held your breath expecting a bullet in the back, for there was only protection from ahead.

'But,' a clearly relieved George recorded, 'nothing happened and I put forward again to look out', before suddenly mentioning for the first time in his archived letters, a certain 'Hamilton', who 'slept night and day. A wonderful man.' Was this none other than the commander-in-chief himself?

They arrived alongside the *Ramazan* around 4am 'after being shifted from every hatch in the ship. Finally she got underway. Towing us and three others alongside, [*she*] made down the coast. I tried to sleep then but gave it up, it being too wet and cold on deck and the hold too horsey.'

About a mile and a half off Anzac, a large shell fell about 30ft from their bow so they weighed anchor and moved another half mile or so further out from the beach.

When George eventually returned to shore he supervised unloading of horses and baggage not to mention some 'natives' apart from one who was, apparently, 'so slow I brought him back'. Thankfully, there was no shelling to contend with this time.

George explained to his father that Anzac beach wasn't 'ideal … owing to a slight swell coming down the coast. If we stayed too long we swung beam on to the beach and most likely became fast aground.'

Then it was back yet again to the *Ramazan* to collect yet another cargo of mules before setting off once more with also a lighter in tow. This, complained George, 'was the second time we towed a lighter and it was hardly fair to us for we had our work cut out to care for ourselves.'

The donkey work, literally, undertaken by Unwin and George, among others, was noted admiringly by Admiral Keyes in his memoir: 'It would be impossible to exaggerate the furious energy which was put into the disembarkation of artillery, mules etc., etc., by Unwin and the people working with him and on the beaches. I counted 127 mules come out of the hold and off the upper deck of one lighter designed to carry 50 at the most. They worked incessantly …'

Now, wrote George, 'we tried a little higher up with some success as far as getting into the beach. The natives were slow … and we began to swing so rapidly that I had to kick them ashore and throw their baggage after them. We backed out after hoisting the brow but one silly fool left his bag, and when we got clear he was found hanging on to the brow. I took him on, however.'

Unlike their last foray to Anzac, there was now some fierce shelling to deal with: 'Whiz bangs and shrapnel from both sides. When we were about a mile from the beach, Hamilton was hunting around the deck for pieces of shell when he suddenly jumped and asked, "Who the hell's throwing stones at me?"

'He hopped down below and on taking his boot off found a hole through his foot before the ankle. He fainted soon after so I caught a picket boat and put him aboard the *Bacchante* ... being the nearest ship. It was evidently a shell splinter though nobody noticed it coming.

'Afterwards I found the sacking round our desk ballast had smouldered away. Two or three miles on I met K-6 bound for Anzac. I told him the way, gave him the native and told him what a nice place it was. He seemed to be suffering from lack of sleep and had lost his voice. I reported Hamilton to HMS *Jonquil* and received orders to load from the *Dundrennan* ... a nice clean ship, no mules about her.'

As there appears to be no actual evidence that Sir Ian Hamilton, although in the vicinity, ever suffered an actual injury during the campaign, let alone during the Suvla landing, one has, a little sadly, to conclude that this particular 'Hamilton' must remain an anonymous shipmate of considerably lesser rank that the great man.

George had been on his feet for more than thirty hours and now firmly resisted all efforts to make him stow yet more cargo, especially as there was already a party from a man-of-war working in two watches on that very task. He joined all hands for a swim 'to keep awake but the current was too strong to stay more than a minute or two'.

It was 4pm when, with the cargo half-loaded, Commander Unwin suddenly arrived on the *Dundrennan* and informed George he had another job for him. They left together in a large open motorboat. After three hours and finding themselves nearby the hospital ship *Soudan*, they went aboard for dinner, leaving just a couple of hours later with a party of soldiers destined for A Beach, 'going on a rock as we went in but doing no damage,' George noted, blithely, of yet another non-fatal accident in his already mishap-strewn existence.

Next port-of-call was HMS *Swiftsure*, a pre-dreadnought battleship, tying up at around 11pm and where, wrote George, 'I lost no time and slept on the deck.'

Swiftsure would now remain his base for the next 48 hours or so, hours punctuated by a further series of alarms and excursions for the young midshipman, starting again shortly after 5am on the morning of 10 August when he and the equally tireless Unwin 'shoved along to various ships and lighters. The time passed quickly and so did my breakfast for I did not get any.'

As they approached the *Ikalis*, an armed merchantman, they spotted a pair of 'Beetles' on either side of the ship. As they moved around *Ikalis*, a great 'Bang!' rang out. A shell had hit the ship, killed two on one of the lighters and wounded two more. George was ordered to ferry the fatalities to A Beach for immediate burial.

Returning to *Swiftsure* he learned to his great delight he had become an 'honorary member' of the ship's mess with a decent lunch as his first reward. He spent the rest of the afternoon towing soldiers ashore before re-joining Unwin that evening for another hop into A Beach, where – surprise, surprise – they encountered exactly the same rock as during the day, only this time actually 'holing' the vessel so they had to abandon it on the beach, leaving two men in charge.

Back on *Swiftsure* at 11pm, George 'slung a hammock and had a jolly good sleep'. After breakfast the following morning, he returned to A Beach and 'found the two fools had let the water rise and my camera was ruined'. They baled her out and towed her back to *Swiftsure* where she was hoisted.

George spent the rest of the day aboard the battleship until 7pm when he was required to search for some paraffin oil on one of the lighters which was finally located at A Beach. It was getting towards midnight when he finally returned to the ship for the night 'and another good sleep'.

Of Thursday 12 August, George told his father: 'I nearly turned into a soldier. [I] was going with some Naval guns but,' he recorded with obvious disappointment but no specific reason, 'it all fell through.' The simplest explanation was that he'd been ordered to report back to his own ship, *Hussar*, after more than a week of colourful Suvla adventures.

He wrote that he could have remained on the beaches with Unwin, who had now been officially appointed beachmaster for the duration, but for an order that no midshipmen were to go ashore – presumably for a lengthy period – unless inoculated. He then added: 'Anyhow, I have been inoculated since, but I don't like the beach in rainy weather.

'This ends the Suvla landing as I saw it,' concluded George, VC-elect, in his third and final letter home dated 12 November 1915, more than three months after his final departure from the sector.

Well, not quite. In his final observations, George noted that a mere half hour after he'd left *Swiftsure*, the battleship was 'strafed badly and she had to shift billet'. What George didn't know at the time – or maybe even censored later to conceal – was that *Swiftsure* had been severely battered by an enemy field gun, a 12-pounder. She was hit ten times, resulting in five killed and ten wounded.

What George's letters also don't convey, apart from continuing to demonstrate graphically, even on occasion nonchalantly, the art of personal survival, was the increasingly chaotic aggregation all over the peninsula of command blunder, pestilence, disease, misery, blood-letting and death that would dog the campaign almost from first to last.

Heroism was, of course, ever-present during all of those eight or so months, although it's intriguing to note that of the thirty-nine VCs awarded during the campaign, less than a half would emanate as a result of military actions following the Suvla landings, which occurred almost exactly halfway though the Dardanelles timeline. Heroism fatigue?

Of the half a million men sent by the Allies to Gallipoli during the 259 days of the campaign – between the first landing in April and the final withdrawal in January 1916 – more than fifty per cent became casualties, fractionally more than those suffered in total by the Turks.

Higher-profile Allied 'casualties' during the conflict included Winston Churchill who was demoted from First Lord of the Admiralty in May (before resigning entirely from Government in November) and

Sir Ian Hamilton, who was recalled to London in October and replaced as commander-in-chief by Sir Charles Munro.

After the extreme heat of the summer and its attendant ills had been brutally replaced by flood, mud, blizzards and freeze with their own horrific accessories from late autumn into gathering winter, it was clearly time for a carefully-planned evacuation, which, writes historian Peter Doyle, 'despite dire warnings to the contrary … would be hailed as one of the greatest feats of any military campaign – the lifting of so many troops from under the noses of the enemy.' Or, as *The Times* bellowed it on 21 December: *'The most astonishingly successful withdrawal in the whole history of war.'*

George's old captain was there almost to the end, heroic to a fault. As Keyes wrote in his memoir, referring to General Julian Byng who was now supervising the withdrawal: 'When I saw Byng after the evacuation he told me that on the way off in the last boat from Suvla, a soldier fell overboard and Unwin jumped in and saved his life. He said, "You must really do something about Unwin. You should send him home; we want several little Unwins."'

In all, some 142,000 men were evacuated by early January 1916 with, it has been claimed, just three casualties when official estimates had cited possibly up to 30,000.

Shortly before the peninsula had been finally shed of Allied troops, *The Times* cautioned:

> *But having congratulated ourselves upon a fortunate escape from the more dangerous section of the positions at Gallipoli, there is still a reckoning to be made. This is not, perhaps, the time to make it, but those responsible may be quite certain that the nation will not be content to regard the Dardanelles undertaking as a closed incident.*

After enumerating the human casualty list up to some six weeks or so before publication, *The Times* continued to pursue its grim accounting:

We have also lost various battleships and other vessels, have spent an incredible amount of money, and have nothing to show in return except the imperishable records of the heroism of our soldiers and sailors.

All that can be done now is to note the various questions upon which further explanation is unquestionably due … Associated with these issues is the very grave question of what happened at the Suvla Bay landing and at the disastrous failure to make good the advance a fortnight later.

Reflecting the concerns of millions at home, including George's family, for whom Gallipoli might have seemed, at first, a distant sideshow compared with the neighbouring slaughter just across the Channel, *The Times* urged the Government to publish Sir Ian Hamilton's promised Third Despatch on the campaign without *'any avoidable delay'*. This, the newspaper suggested, might help *'allocate responsibility for the faulty inception and blundering execution of one of the most monumental failures with which British arms have ever been associated.'*

As George, still aboard *Hussar* at year's end, continued to patrol the North Aegean, another Navy man, Ordinary Seaman Joe Murray of Hood Battalion, Royal Naval Division, mused poignantly – as quoted by Max Arthur – 'I thought to myself, "I don't like sneaking away like this after all this bloody trouble." I was really distressed in my own mind. I thought to myself, "We're stealing away. We stole away from Blandford, stole away from Egypt and now we're stealing away from Gallipoli …" I remember how happy and anxious we were to get stuck into the Turks. And now here we were, only a handful left.'

Left behind forever were the dead, known, unknown, on land and at sea. On 28 October Second Lieutenant Hamo Watts Sassoon of the Royal Engineers was hit in the leg by a sniper at Suvla Bay. He was transferred to a nearby hospital ship, the SS *Kildonan Castle*, where it was feared his leg would have to be amputated. However, the wound had already become septic and he died, four days later on 1 November. Sassoon, aged 26, was buried at sea.

His older brother, Siegfried, serving at the time with conspicuous bravery on the Western Front, was perhaps echoing many other grieving siblings when he wrote:

> *Give me your hand, my brother, search my face;*
> *Look in these eyes lest I should think of shame;*
> *For we have made an end of all things base.*
> *We are returning by the road we came.*

> *Your lot is with the ghosts of soldiers dead,*
> *And I am in the field where men must fight.*
> *But in the gloom I see your laurell'd head*
> *And through your victory I shall win the light.*

Alan Moorehead wrote in his account of Gallipoli, first published in 1956: 'In the face of so much mismanagement things were bound to go wrong, yet not so wrong as all this … And yet it was quite unlike the April landing. One does not have the feeling it was touch and go at Suvla, that some shifting of the pattern would have put things right again. There is instead a strong sense of inevitability; each event leads on quite inexorably to the next, and it cannot have mattered, one feels, whether Hamilton went to bed or not, whether the brigadiers marched in this or that direction – the results would have been just the same. Given this set of conditions everything was bound to continue to its fated end.'

The apportioning of blame continues to echo down the years. In his memoir of the campaign, published in 1924, Lord Wester-Wemyss suggested, 'the blame for this tragedy cannot be laid at the door of any one individual, but must be attributed to the system, the system that places the direction of naval and military operation solely in the hands of men devoid of the knowledge and experience necessary for the task, and immune, moreover, from the consequences of their action.'

More specifically, he derided 'the lack of vision and incapacity of our politicians'.

Well he would, wouldn't he? What must be absolutely undeniable is that militarily, at least, the enemy – the so-called 'sick man of Europe' – had been almost wilfully, some might even suggest, criminally, underestimated.

In his 'official' history, published between 1929 and 1932, Brigadier General C.F. Aspinall-Oglander, who arrived at Suvla Bay on the third day, opined, sternly: 'By the hesitation and delay of the 7th and 8th August, the advantages gained by the surprise landing at Suvla had all but been thrown away. The IX Corps had trifled too long with time. The chance of gaining the high ground on very easy terms had disappeared. It was now to be a fight between forces of equal numbers, with the British troops in the open, sun-baked plain, and the Turks in possession of every point of vantage. The Turks, moreover, were definitely superior in skirmishing and in the use of their rifles to these young New Army troops straight out from England, and once surprise had gone there was little chance with anything approaching equal numbers of scoring a British success.'

When Churchill produced his own extremely readable, but inevitably loaded, account of the Great War in 'about 24 fortnightly parts' (it finally stretched to twenty-six), he pronounced, with considerable hindsight: 'The campaign of the Dardanelles had been starved and crippled at every stage by the continued opposition of the French and British High Commands in France to the withdrawal of troops and munitions from the main theatre of war,' concluding that 'the final decision to evacuate Gallipoli at the time when the position of the Turkish army was most desperate and the British Navy most confident,' was a 'tragedy'.

Ninety years on, in his own Gallipoli history, first published in 2011, Peter Hart draws together bluntly the military and political with this terse summation: 'Thanks to political interference, lethally combined with the bullish optimism of generals who only saw opportunities, the Gallipoli campaign was launched into a void that guaranteed failure.'

They left many traps that exploded in their trenches when we went into them. All this was an unnecessary unkindness. They blew up their stores on the beach, but there was still enough equipment left for we who remained to take two years to collect it all. This included the bully beef that neither we nor they liked very much. In their trenches some soldiers had left tricks for us, such as rum bottles filled with paraffin, but others had left meals for us, set out on plates, and they left messages for us. Obviously I couldn't read them, but I was told they said things like "Goodbye Johnny Turk, thank you for respecting the Red Cross, and remember that it was us who left, it wasn't you who pushed us out." I have a piece of paper that is now very old and yellow, and apparently it says, "Goodbye, Abdul."

Louis de Bernières, *Birds Without Wings*

Chapter 9

A Family at War

We have now been in the trenches under shot and shell for ten days,
and it's something terrible I give you my word and no mistake. The
noise is absalutely deafening. Enough to make your hair curl. We do
not get a moment's sleep all night. We are now well in for it with the
Terrible Turk, who by all accounts is a proper Bugar and no mistake.
No more bloody armies for me. The next bloody army I join is the
Salvation bloody army and don't you forget it.

– a letter home from Gallipoli

The Great War was littered with family tragedies, none more poignant
than the multiple loss of siblings, sometimes as many as up to five sons
sacrificed from a single household. According to historian Anthony
Seldon: 'No records were kept at the time of how many brothers were
killed, or indeed how many fathers and sons, and only now are we able
to ascertain the full extent of these multiple disasters for families. In
the Gallipoli campaign, no fewer than 196 pairs of brothers were killed.
Of that total of 392 men, only thirteen have marked graves.'

Thomas and Mary Ann Drewry must have been typical of so many
parents who had to look on helplessly as their offspring, spanning a
decade in age range, were all, at one time or another, 'in harm's way'
between 1914 and 1918.

Towards the end of May 1916, with George now promoted to acting
sub-lieutenant on *Hussar* and docked safely for some days at Port Said,
his oldest brother, Harry, was aboard HMS *Princess Royal* in the North
Sea shortly to be embroiled in the most celebrated naval battle of the
Great War.

Before being called up to the RNR eight months earlier, Harry, a marine engineer like his father, had served for five years as an apprentice engineer with P&O, appearing in the company's seniority lists as, first, 'an assistant engineer', then, 'fourth engineer', between 1909 and 1913.

After that he worked for the Haslam Foundry and Engineering Company in Derby before moving on to the Edinburgh-based Brown Brothers, most famous for ship steering gear, used by liners, ferries and, of course, Navy vessels. Latterly, Brown's had also moved into the manufacture of artillery shells for the war effort.

With the rank of engineer sub-lieutenant, 26-year-old Harry, now based at the home station HMS *Victory*, Portsmouth was sent over three successive weeks on a series of short courses – in oil fuel, turbines and engines – before finally joining his ship for temporary service on 29 October, 1915.

Until then, the battlecruiser *Princess Royal* had, under the overall command of Osmond Brock, taken part in both of the war's earlier North Sea encounters – at Heligoland Bight in August, 1914, and off Dogger Bank the following January – but neither encounter, despite being technically British victories, would prove decisive in the ongoing sea war.

In the last week of May, naval intelligence, forewarned by the chattering radios of German U-boats moving into position off British ports, alerted Admiral Jellicoe, Commander-in-Chief of the Grand Fleet stationed at Scapa Flow in the Orkneys and Vice Admiral Beatty, Commander of the First Battlecruiser Squadron docked at Rosyth on the Firth of Forth, that something 'big' was brewing.

On 31 May, they and their German counterparts, Admiral Scheer, who commanded the High Seas Fleet, and Beatty's old adversary, Vice Admiral von Hipper, Commander of Scouting Forces, were ranged against each other on a dreary afternoon for what would be the last ever major battle to be fought between fleets of battleships.

What happened next at Jutland off the west coast of Denmark tends to vary in the telling.

Basil Liddell Hart's *History of the First World War*, first published in 1930, provides a rather whimsical summation of the events: of the two opposing fleets, he wrote, 'it would be more exact to say they hailed each other in passing – with a hail that was awe-inspiring but leaving an impression that was merely pen-inspiring. No battle in history has spilt so much – ink ... the fleet that had been built to dispute the mastery of the sea stumbled into the fleet that had held it for centuries. In the early evening these two fleets, the greatest the world had seen, groped towards each other, touched, broke away, touched again and broke away again. And when the glorious First of June dawned a sorely puzzled Grand Fleet paraded on an empty sea.'

Seventy years later, John Keegan would write in a rather less opaque way of Jutland in his own acclaimed history of the Great War: 'That it was a British victory of some sort is not now denied. That it was less than a decisive victory is not denied either. It was the disparity between British expectations of victory and the success actually achieved that led to the detailed dissection of the battle's events and the controversy that persists to this day. The Royal Navy, undefeated in a major fleet action since Trafalgar, sailed for Jutland in the sure belief that, should a junction of battle fleets ensue, another Trafalgar would occur. The inconclusiveness of the event has continued to haunt the mind of the Royal Navy ever since.'

From Harry's perspective on *Princess Royal*, one of six battlecruisers in Beatty's squadron, such cool considerations couldn't have been further from his, or anyone's, mind, from the moment first shots were fired at 3.48pm. Within three minutes *Princess Royal*, under its flag captain Walter Cowan, had sustained two severe hits. This resulted in the ship's 'A' turret – one of four, housing two guns each – from working effectively. The turret's left gun became inoperable while the right gun misfired frequently. At 4.11, a German torpedo from SMS *Moltke* passed under the ship.

Less than half an hour later, two of Beatty's ships, *Indefatigable* and *Queen Mary*, had been sunk with the catastrophic loss of more than

2,200 lives. Beatty's own flagship *Lion* was only saved from possibly the same fate by the quick thinking of a brave Marine, Major Francis Harvey, who, just before he died, ordered the flooding of its magazines after a German shell from *Lützow*, her opposite number in the enemy formation, had struck the midship 'Q' turret. For his action Major Harvey was to earn a posthumous VC.

For some moments shortly after 4.35pm, it seemed that Harry and his ship had also become another disastrous casualty of war. Around the time *Queen Mary* was going to her watery grave marked by a huge pall of smoke, reportedly 800ft high, *Princess Royal* suddenly vanished from sight in a cloud of smoke and spray. A signalman on *Lion* reported, '*Princess Royal* blown up', leading Beatty to utter, testily, to his flag captain the famous line, 'Chatfield, there seems to be something wrong with our bloody ships today.'

Once the smoke and spray had cleared, it was, thankfully, plain to see that *Princess Royal* was safe after all.

After a series of manoeuvres, first south, then north, then north-east, by Beatty's squadron – now reduced from six battlecruisers to four – battle recommenced around 5.40pm. Forty minutes later, *Princess Royal* was hit again, this time by two 305mm shells, which disabled its 'X' turret and penetrated the ship's side armour.

For *Princess Royal*, the battle continued on and, mostly, off over the next several hours in first, haze and, then, increasingly poor visibility. By the late evening, Beatty's battlecruisers were sailing south south-east ahead of both the Grand Fleet and High Seas Fleet until the order was finally given, at 2.55am, to reverse course and head for home, reaching Rosyth the following day. *Princess Royal* was hit, in total, nine times during the Battle of Jutland, leaving nineteen killed and eighty-one injured.

The ship's log remains curiously sketchy in its record of the action: '3.45 open fire', '9.05 ceased fire' with scant detail in between. 'Passed by quantity of wreckage including hammocks and dead body', and 'committed 19 bodies to the deep' is about as colourful as it gets.

As Harry mourned his dead shipmates – ranging in age from 19-year-old able seamen to a 38-year-old gunner, not to mention the canteen manager and his assistant – it's worth reflecting that *Princess Royal's* human loss represented only a tiny percentage of the overall British dead. At 6,094 it was more than twice the number of Germans, as well as, in terms of shipping, almost double the tonnage of the enemy in this so-called Allied victory.

Perhaps the most celebrated British casualty of Jutland was Jack 'Boy' Cornwell, a sight setter who was fatally wounded after remaining at his post aboard the light cruiser, HMS *Chester*, which had been hit by fire from four German cruisers. Cornwell, who'd joined the Royal Navy in 1915 without getting parental permission, was only 16 when he died two days later after his stricken ship reached port. He received a posthumous VC – a second such award for an East London boy as the Cornwell family lived less than two miles from the Drewry home.

'But if,' concludes Liddell Hart, darkly, 'discounting all criticisms, we admit that Jellicoe's handling of the battle fleet was the flawless masterpiece that numerous naval admirers argue, the admission only strengthens the belief that the worst fault of the Jutland battle was that it was ever fought.'

George, who less than a year earlier, had participated in two other of the Great War's more futile clashes some 1,000 miles to the south east of his older brother, might well have concurred with that sentiment.

At Rosyth, *Princess Royal* underwent eight days of temporary repairs before sailing for Plymouth where more permanent repairs were effected on the damaged battlecruiser. By 21 July, the ship had returned to Rosyth. A week later Harry received news of his promotion to engineer lieutenant.

Harry might have survived – and he even returned with an inscribed fragment of armour shell, courtesy of the German battleship *Markgraf* – but some notes in the Drewry/Kendall family archive suggest that his health was affected from Jutland onwards.

Closeted throughout the entire battle in one of the ship's two engine rooms housing direct-drive steam turbines, Harry would later tell his family that it was 'hell not knowing what was going to happen, shut off, and stokers cursing like mad in the heat keeping up maximum steam for speed'.

Harry's pre- and post-Jutland service on *Princess Royal* consisted of uneventful North Sea patrols but mostly in port at either Rosyth or Scapa Flow, apart from one ship-heavy sortie, in August 1916, after naval intelligence suggested that Scheer's High Seas Fleet was leaving harbour to bombard Sunderland on Britain's north-east coast. The rival fleets never in fact engaged although two British light cruisers were sunk in the process by German submarines.

Not long before the first anniversary of Jutland, Harry wrote to Aunt Eleanor from Rosyth:

Many thanks for your letter of 23rd inst. I should have answered it more promptly only I dropped in for a spot of work on my return and then caught a chill which sent me to roost. Anyhow, I am glad to say that I am alright again and we have settled down for a few more months of war, such as it is.

They tell me from home that Ma is at Gy [Grimsby] and as I haven't heard from her for some time, I presume she is having a good time. For the last week the weather here has been very bleak and cold and it doesn't look at all promising for the allotment holders although one of our officers informed me this morning that his first potato plant had appeared above ground.

This is Saturday afternoon and incidentally, my day aboard for duty so I have been employing the shining hour, or rather hours, in yelling or trying to fill in my income tax return. I declare that the forms get more complicated each year; someone has got to pay for the war though and my little bit will not keep it going many seconds but I suppose it will all help.

I have been quite a social bird lately attending two Sunday afternoon tea fights since I returned and talked "hot air" while I balanced a cup of tea on my knee. Am glad to hear that Ronald has taken up cycling and hope that he gets plenty of pleasure out of it; you certainly have fine roads of country in Lincolnshire.

3.30pm or seven bells has just struck and the rattle of tea cups and alleged cake calls me, so must close before my hungry mess mates finish everything up before I get there. Please give my love to Ronald. With all the best wishes to Uncle D.

Your affectionate nephew, Harry

Ronald was Harry's young cousin.

In the course of his time on *Princess Royal*, Harry earned many plaudits on his service record. Typically: 'zealous and trustworthy', wrote Captain Cowan, adding, 'a good watchkeeper and suitable for permanent [Navy] list'.

From the middle of 1917, with a good shore job for the future assured as an engineer representative with Messrs Buck & Hickman Ltd, a long established major tools distributor, Harry still had to keep 'civvy street' on hold as he was now required to help with the building of an Anchusa-class sloop, HMS *Spiraea*, out of Devonport. *Spiraea* was one of twenty-eight such sloops – a single screw fleet sweeping vessel – built under the Emergency War Programme for the Navy.

Although he had applied for release from the Navy, his record noted 'cannot be spared at present', later observing, 'this officer was appointed to the ship when building to supervise the engines and auxiliary machinery. Has justified the confidence placed in him and proved an efficient trustworthy Engineer Officer since commissioning.'

Finally, on 1 August 1919, he was demobilized, his record later stating that 'he does not desire to be considered for appointment to the Special Reserve of Engineer Officers of the RN'. After more than three years on active service in the Navy, Harry was well and truly done with the sea.

Meanwhile, George's post-Dardanelles service on *Hussar* continued, contrasting starkly with his brief but eventful days of front line action in April and August 1915. The logs spell out just an endless round of pootling about the Aegean and Mediterranean, sailing in and out of familiar ports like Salonika, Mudros, Kondia (further west on Lemnos) for the odd game of cricket, Salonika, Milos, Syra, Suda Bay (on the north-west coast of Crete), Kephalo, Leros, Salamis (just off the Greek mainland) and, just occasionally, Malta and Port Said.

From 1914 onwards, his commanding officer reports had been consistently first rate: 'To my entire satisfaction as a very capable watchkeeper, very zealous, keen and promises very well' to 'very hard-working & reliable and above average both in ability and neatness'. Commander Unwin had noted, soberly: 'Entire satisfaction and of great assistance to me in *River Clyde*' while a later skipper, Captain Giffard, offered, 'very reliable and steady', adding, usefully, 'service in a ship of the line in Grand Fleet would be of great value to him. This suggestion is not meant in any way to the detriment of the gallant, able, young officer.'

In December 1916, Giffard's 'suggestion' happily came to fruition when, after a couple of months at HMS *Excellent*, the Portsmouth home base and gunnery school, George was transferred to HMS *Conqueror*.

Conqueror, launched in 1911, was an Orion-class dreadnought battleship assigned to the Home and Grand Fleets. Sometimes called a 'super dreadnought' because of its size, the ship boasted heavy armour and ten 13.5-inch guns, as well as a huge crew of more than 750 officers and ratings. Yet, despite its size and strength, *Conqueror* enjoyed, if that's the right word, remarkably little wartime action up to and after George's assignment to the vessel.

She began the war as part of the Home Fleet stationed at Scapa Flow, then in November took part in what proved to a fruitless sweep of the southern part of the North Sea following reports of German submarine action. A month later, in mid-December, she headed out to sea again as part of a large force in what proved to be a failed attempt to intercept enemy ships after they'd successfully bombarded England's north-east coast, principally Scarborough, Hartlepool and Whitby.

Later the same month, *Conqueror* did manage to make close contact with another ship. Unfortunately, it was a fellow dreadnought battleship HMS *Monarch* which she accidentally rammed while they were both returning to Scapa Flow in a force ten gale. A year and a half on, at Jutland, as the seventh ship from the head of the battle line, *Conqueror* was reported to have fired some fifty-seven 12-inch shells without registering a single hit.

Her log records that at 1pm on 28 December, 'Sub-Lieut Drewry VC RNR joined the ship'. But if George, who'd received his promotion in September, thought that a step up from the torpedo gunboat *Hussar* to a full-blown battleship would somehow satisfy what would be noted officially as his keen desire 'for active service' then he'd be sorely disappointed.

For the next eleven months aboard *Conqueror*, George spent his time, for the most part, looking out over Scapa Flow and its Grand Fleet anchorage. There were occasional sorties: to the North Sea for routine patrols, and the Pentland Firth, that occasionally fearsome strait between the Orkneys and the north coast of Scotland, for night firing. But otherwise it was mostly mundane duties, supervising painting, cleaning and gyro checking.

However, on 9 July 1917, George would likely have been a witness to one of the Great War's more bizarre disasters. A little over a year after Lord Kitchener was killed, along with 737 others, after the armoured cruiser HMS *Hampshire* struck German mines off the western side of Orkney, the battleship HMS *Vanguard* blew up at her moorings in the northern part of Scapa Flow. The huge internal explosion at around 11.20pm, emanating from the ship's own ordnance, claimed 843 men in all. The toll would have been greater had not some officers been attending a concert on another ship at the time.

Although some key battles of the Western Front took place less than 150 miles from London, it is all too easy to imagine that in these still early days of aviation and the unlikely eventuality of enemy invasion, the capital was somehow immune from the realities of front line warfare.

But as Ralph, the youngest of the Drewry brothers, and his parents in Forest Gate would find out, that was far from the case on the Home Front, especially east of London. Ralph, 16 when war broke out, was employed as an apprentice boilermaker/plater with P&O, refitting ships and doing, according to his own short memoir compiled later for his family, 'a man's job owing to the shortage of labour, working overtime every day up to 9.30pm from 7am, and also on Sundays'.

His day often didn't end there for Ralph was regularly on rooftop night duty fire-watching during Zeppelin attacks. The first Zeppelin raids took place in January 1915 on coastal towns in East Anglia before adding London as a regular target over the next two years. In all, there were fifty-two such raids on Britain during the war, killing over 500 people.

Then, on 19 January 1917, a few months before George was probably an unwitting witness to an accidental disaster up in Orkney, so Ralph must also have had almost a front row seat to the infamous 'Silvertown Explosion' less than half a mile from the Royal Docks. Seventy-three people died, more than 400 were injured, and no fewer than 70,000 buildings were destroyed or damaged when 50 tons of TNT, destined for munitions in the trenches, blew up in the factory of Brunner, Mond and Co.

Aerial attacks escalated as the enemy introduced its Gotha IV bi-plane bombers which undertook eight deadly daylight raids between May and August 1917. The worst of three on London occurred on 25 May when, in Poplar, barely two miles from the Drewry home, 162 people were killed, including eighteen primary schoolchildren.

Percy was still working for P&O in Kobe when war broke out. Officially an ally of Britain since 1902, Japan declared war on Germany on 23 August and the Austria-Hungary two days later. Ambitious to be a significant colonial power, Japan quickly and successfully made a move on Germany's Pacific territories and, for the rest of the war, with and without one or other of the Allies' approval, aimed to increase its sphere of influence, notably in China.

Despite a note in the Drewry/Kendall family archive indicating that Percy returned to Europe soon after hostilities began, more reliable sources suggest that he remained in the Far East until at least towards the end of 1917 before heading back home. In ships' passenger records of the time, he was listed as 'single' on 23 January 1918, when travelling from Hong Kong to Vancouver. A little over two months later, his Navy Service Record logs him, from 1 April, as a temporary sub-lieutenant with the Royal Navy Volunteer Reserve.

That same day, Percy, aged 28, was assigned to HMS *President*, a shore establishment on the Thames responsible for the administration of naval personnel assigned for miscellaneous duties. There he learned he'd been appointed to the staff of the Principal Naval Transport Officer for duty in Bordeaux, presumably a result of his years of experience with P&O. The task of the PNTO was principally to transport entire crews to and from England to keep the local ships on station. Although he was demobilized just a year later, Percy had by then initiated a significant French connection, which, as we'll learn later, would lead on in due course to a life of considerable wealth and comfort.

While Percy was still travelling back from the Far East, George, now an acting lieutenant, had swapped the North Sea and *Conqueror* for assignment to HMS *Research*, stationed at Portland, one of the largest man-made harbours in the world, off the Channel coast of Dorset. The Chatham-built paddle survey vessel was now employed as a depot ship for, among other things, training Navy personnel like George in the use of fish hydrophones for submarine detection.

After six weeks intensive instruction in trying to combat the continuing threat of German U-boats, which had already been successful across four years in sinking a considerable tonnage of Navy and merchant shipping, George travelled north again, this time to assume his first command, at 23, of His Majesty's Trawler, *William Jackson*.

> *The silence bade me look towards Troy across the Straits from Helles,*
> *I still could hear no voice, nor thunder in the sky except the launching*
> *waves pushing ancient pebbles up the beach to rest, where once they*
> *drowned the hearts of men.*
>
> Michael J. Whelan

Chapter 10

On Active Service

There is an old saying in the Navy that seniority among midshipmen does not count and that the most suitable get the best jobs.
Captain Eric Bush DSO DSC RN

From his appointment on 11 March 1918 as skipper of HMT *William Jackson* up to and including his untimely death that August, there continues to be a shroud of mystery over those last four months or so in George's short, accident-prone life, so some of the following, it has to be admitted, is a careful blend of fact and some speculation, finely spiced with just a jot of confusion.

Some seven years before the outbreak of hostilities, Admiral Lord Charles Beresford had recommended that steam trawlers be used in the role of minesweepers in the event of war. Lord Charles, controversial in both his public and private life – a notorious adulterer as well as fiercely ambitious, he yearned unsuccessfully to be First Sea Lord – reasoned this would free up warships for other, more appropriate, duties.

So in 1914 many of Hull's trawlers were requisitioned for minesweeping and anti-submarine duties, around 800 in all from both the Hull and Grimsby fishing fleets, while a new rank, Skipper Royal Naval Reserve, was introduced for trawler skippers.

William Jackson was one of seventy steam trawlers built by Cochrane & Sons specifically for the Royal Navy during the Great War. Founded by Andrew Cochrane in 1884, his shipbuilding business, Cochrane & Sons, moved in 1898 from Beverley in Yorkshire's old West Riding, thirty miles west to Selby, more conveniently sited on the River Ouse, albeit fifty miles from the sea.

According to *Grace's Guide*, the trawlers were 'deployed by the Admiralty as minesweepers, gunboats and barges. The yard was able to achieve such a massive output by building the trawlers ten at a time in five pairs. In addition, the yard was laid out in such a way so that ships could be launched two at a time and construction could take place rotationally, with members of staff working on one task at a time for two weeks before the next task was undertaken.'

Due to its river location, launches were undertaken sideways with, it has been reported, crowds watching excitedly either side of the Ouse, with those on the Barlby bank opposite the shipyard taking care to avoid the inevitable heavy wave as a vessel noisily left the slipway.

Now this is where it starts to get a bit murky. Despite extensive research at the three principal repositories of British naval shipping logs – the National Archives, Kew, the National Maritime Museum, Greenwich, and the Maritime Museum at St John's, Newfoundland – there is simply no log extant for the first few months of *William Jackson*'s service; frustratingly, they are only available for the period beginning more a month <u>after</u> George's death.

It has to be assumed that any earlier log went missing or was destroyed before the surviving logs went into the Admiralty archives, ahead of their being subsequently selected for permanent preservation and transfer to the Public Record Office (later the National Archives).

As far as what would prove to be, sadly, George's short association with the vessel is concerned, 'the log would normally commence,' noted naval historian Steve Hunnisett, 'at the moment the vessel was commissioned – i.e. once she was accepted from her builders and raised the White Ensign for the first time.

'George would have been in command of the ship before her commissioning and would have been paid a nominal sum by her builders for doing so. Until the moment of acceptance by the RN, the vessel technically remains the property of her builders. Once sea trials were successfully completed – in those days, they would basically have consisted of ensuring that everything on board worked correctly, conducting speed trials with the engines etc. [*notably hydrophones*] – he would have formally "signed" for the ship and accepted her into RN service, at which point the White Ensign would be hoisted and the vessel commissioned into the Navy's service.

'At this point a "working up" procedure would then have been carried out over a period of a few weeks (in peacetime a longer operation), which would have basically been to ensure that the ship's officers and company were all proficient in their jobs and in the general operation of the new ship.'

Once the ship and her people had been assessed as capable and competent, she would, an insider at the Naval Historical Branch further clarified, have only then taken up her duties on routine anti-submarine patrol, in this case as part of the Northern Patrol at Scapa Flow in the Orkneys. The patrol was based around the 10th Cruiser Squadron deployed on distant blockade of German maritime trade to and from the continent, detection of armed raiders attempting the northern route into and out of the North Atlantic, and anti-submarine patrols.

So, Hunnisett re-iterated, George would 'almost certainly have taken command of his ship at the builders' yard and signed for her there. The commanding officer always signed for the ship from the builder on satisfactory completion of trials.' That suggests George made his first acquaintance of the 148-foot long, 327 tonne, Mersey-class trawler with its single 12-pounder gun at Selby.

However, George's oldest surviving relative, also called George, his brother Ralph's son, recalls being told once that his uncle actually took command properly of the ship way down river at Hull on the Humber estuary. This seems to make sense, as it's more likely that a sheltered sea environment would be more conducive to sea trials than on an inland river with its limited width, 20 yards at most.

It would also have meant that George, who had been away at war for more than four years almost non-stop, was, for a while at least, within spitting distance of his beloved relatives at Grimsby where he'd spent many precious and memorable holidays in his youth.

If family recollection is correct, George would have set sail on *William Jackson* from Hull on or around Wednesday 31 July ahead of a two-day voyage of just over 320 nautical miles to Scapa Flow. There is a photo of him leaning over the ship's rail, which, according to his great nephew, was taken just two days before his death, presumably just out of port.

His cap firmly fixed, his two lieutenant stripes clearly visible on sleeve, George, looking considerably older and more weathered than his 23 years, also appears to be clutching binoculars. It is a picture relaying assurance and some contentment.

Yet less than forty-eight hours later, on Friday 2 August, George was dead, after accidentally sustaining a fractured skull and a broken left arm.

Next day, following an inquiry held on board the old battleship HMS *Implacable*, now depot ship for the Northern Patrol at Scapa Flow, a report by the ship's chief of staff stated, according to one badly handwritten version of George's navy service record, 'the court found that he was accidentally killed by a boom falling on him. The cause of the boom falling was a flaw in the xxxx of a block.' The word is undecipherable but possibly 'bond'.

Yet, in another version of his service record, also in the files at Kew, the following is scrawled: 'Accidentally killed 2 August 1918 (due to fracture of shackle of topping lift block of after derrick whilst being worked. Derrick fell & struck him on head.'

As if to compound the confusion, there is also extant in the archives, a form declaring 'Casualties – Naval Officers' which records George's place of death as 'at sea. Gallipoli Peninsula', and the cause as 'Accidentally killed' followed by a bizarre conflation of his VC citation, 'under heavy rifle and Maxim fire' with 'due to fracture of shackle etc' as above.

Even odder is the fact that, despite repeated requests, there appears to be no official death certificate for George in existence.

A possible explanation arrived in a response from the organisation, ScotlandsPeople, which administers the National Records of Scotland:

'The information that was recorded during the period of the First World War was not taken down in the way that a conventional death certificate might be, as the recording was not carried out by a registrar but rather by the military clerks.

With so many soldiers being killed in action they would not have the time to check parental details for each man against any documentation that may originally have contained this data, or possibly they did not have that information to hand.

These documents record the demise of each individual as an event, rather than providing the usual background information you might find in a standard statutory record. For this reason the records that you will see in armed forces returns contain scant information, usually only the name, rank, age, service number, place of death and circumstances of the death (if known).'

Whatever the precise sequence or the exact facts of this shipboard calamity were, George is reported to have died just three hours after the incident which, according to family lore, either took place en route to Scapa Flow or once *William Jackson* finally docked in the company of the Grand Fleet.

One would think that the death of a young VC in its waters might have provoked some sort of coverage in the local paper. But a leaf through *The Orcadian*, Orkney's long-established weekly newspaper, for Thursday 8 August, reveals precisely nothing. In between stories about school leaving certificates and 'Splendid Saving Hints for Housewives' there is plenty of war news but whether for censorship or morale reasons, George's passing remained unreported locally. That there is elsewhere a pictorial record of a Royal Navy funeral ceremony at Kirkwall before George's body was transported back south makes the omission even odder.

Coming less than a week after the fourth anniversary of the outbreak of war, which was carefully noted in all the islands' churches, his sacrifice might have seemed the perfect text for such an occasion.

How ironic that of all places Scapa Flow should have proved the scene of his demise for, as has been noted, George had previously spent months and months of relative inactivity as a junior officer on HMS *Conqueror* looking out across this beautiful if bleak anchorage, lying in the middle of Orkney, an archipelago of more than seventy islands – only twenty of which are inhabited – just off the north-eastern tip of Scotland.

Local historian Angus Konstam, a native of Orkney since the age of three, has written of servicemen stationed there complaining in letters home of the loathing they felt for their remote posting and its climate, and the boredom they suffered from.

Derived from Norse words for longboat, isthmus and wide fjord, Scapa Flow had been pondered as a naval base from as early as 1812 before it would eventually serve as such in two twentieth-century world wars, although no defences were actually built before 1914 to protect this natural harbour.

Subsequently, the persistent if rarely realised threat to the anchorage were German U-boats. With its base secure, Konstam has recorded, 'the Navy had little to do but wait for the Germans to make a move. While the smaller ships of the fleet conducted patrols, or hunted for enemy U-boats, the rest of the fleet spent much of the time at anchor inside Scapa Flow, where boredom appeared a far greater enemy than the German fleet.'

Aside from the odd major disaster – *Hampshire* and *Vanguard* notably – surely Scapa's most notorious episode was when, on 21 June 1919, less than a year after George's death, and on the same day the Treaty of Versailles was due to be signed, of the seventy-four German warships interned at Scapa Flow, fifty-two, including fourteen battleships, were suddenly scuttled despite the presence of Royal Navy guard ships.

Weighed against such major seagoing debacles, the freakish circumstances of George's death aboard *William Jackson* must seem positively banal by comparison, but the poignancy of his passing after such a short but still utterly memorable life, and just months before the Armistice, is undeniable. Even the official expression 'died at sea while on active service' takes on a rather hollow ring when contrasted with George's adventures at Gallipoli just three years earlier.

Those were restored to finest relief during a memorial service at evensong held for George at All Saints Church, Forest Gate, on 11 August, just nine days after his death. Here Canon Morrow spoke of the 'pathos of those who laid down their lives when that victory, which they had all longed for, was not yet accomplished. Their history,' he reminded the congregation, 'seemed to be summed up in the text "these all died in faith not having received the promises, but having greeted them from afar,"' a text taken from Hebrews Ch.11.v13.

In a report of the service in the *Stratford Express* a week later, it was said the good Canon drew:

> ... *a pathetic connection between this thought and the death of Lieutenant Drewry who had been laid to rest with all the simplicity which often marked greatness. Little did they think when, two years ago, they met him in the Parochial Hall and presented him with a barograph as a token of esteem and admiration for his magnificent gallantry, that he would be called while yet a mere stripling to a higher service and greater reward.*
>
> *Their consolation lay in the fact that he was one of them, that his name, which already figured largely in the history of the Gallipoli landing would be enshrined on the memorial in All Saints Church. His life was marked by a singular modesty and nobility of character.*

The local paper coverage didn't mention any contribution by the family but in a scribbled note 'from his brothers' headed 'Obituary Notice', one finds the following sentiment:

George was more unaffected by all his deeds and honours than anyone else in our memory. It is sad to think that he should meet his death after going through so many dangers by what must be described as an accident. But it was while on a most important mission of active service which was of incalculable value to our shipping.

Whether this was inserted in the paper separately and/or also read out at the service is not clear but, despite the studied formality of the wording, the affection for, and pride in, their late sibling is still very touching.

George was buried at the City of London Cemetery the day before the memorial service, less than two miles from the church, after his coffin was borne by a horse-drawn carriage, followed by mourners on foot, led by his father and brother Ralph.

Opened in the mid 1800s, the 200-acre cemetery is said to still be the largest such municipal facility in the UK and probably in Europe. He lies among a motley selection of the famous and infamous including two victims of Jack the Ripper, Churchill's nanny, the actress Dame Anna Neagle and footballer Bobby Moore. He also joined another earlier recipient of the VC, Private John Joseph Sims who, at 19, braved heavy fire at Sebastopol during the Crimean War to rescue wounded soldiers, returning them to the trenches, and survived to tell the tale.

Ten months later, on Sunday, 15 June 1919, Canon Morrow was back on Drewry duty at All Saints Church leading an evening service during which was celebrated the installation in the Lady Chapel of a beautiful new stained glass window dedicated to George. It depicted Christ, 'The Light of the World', holding a lantern and awaiting the opening of a door. Immediately below are the words, 'Behold I stand at the door and knock'.

At the foot of the representation is the following inscription:

'To the memory of George Leslie Drewry VC Lieutenant RNR accidentally killed on active service in command of HMS *William*

Jackson on August 2, 1918, aged 23 years. He won the VC in Gallipoli at the landing on V Beach from HMT *River Clyde* April 25 & 26 1915. Erected by his brother officers of the Northern Patrol.'

The Lady Chapel proves to be, in fact, a substantial repository of Drewry family memorials. In addition to George's single window there is also a three-part stained window dedicated to Thomas, Mary Ann and Harry Kendall erected in 1938, as well as two plaques mentioning the four of them, variously. In addition, the three older brothers all feature on one of two Great War commemoration boards either side of the church's main door.

At the time of writing, the church was due for imminent demolition to make way for a new building on the same site. All the stained glass windows will, it's understood, be utilized in the framework of the new structure.

Just before Christmas 1918, it was reported that a Liverpool ship owner, who wanted to remain anonymous, had commissioned a special war medallion in bronze to commemorate the VC men of the *River Clyde*, to be designed by E. Carter Preston, who was also responsible for the National Memorial War Plaque.

The medallion itself was nearly 6ins in diameter and contained four circles looped together depicting a lion rampant, a kangaroo, a cock and an anchor. Attached to each circle were the regimental badges of the Royal Dublin Fusiliers, the West Riding Field Co RE, the Royal Munster Fusiliers and the 2nd Hampshire Regiment. The outer and inner legends were inscribed with the six names, three in each; George between Tisdall and Samson on the inner. The reverse bore a view of the starboard bow of the ship with troops running down the side into landing boats; above, on deck, Maxim guns firing. An inscription read: 'V Beach Landing Dardanelles April 25 1915'.

There were, of course, only three of the six still alive at the time of commission and the medallions were entrusted to the Imperial Merchant Service Guild for eventual presentation. However, there seems to be no record of the Drewry family ever receiving the award.

After the war, George's ship was refurbished as a Hull-based fishing trawler and renamed *Lord Byng* before being sold again in 1936 when she was re-named *Evelyn Rose*, operating out of Fleetwood as a fishery protection vessel.

During the Second World War she helped disembark troops from Dunkirk then, on her return to Ramsgate struck a wreck, lost a propeller blade and was badly damaged in an air attack. Resuming fishing duties in the late 1940s, she eventually, in 1954, foundered in the Sound of Mull. An inquiry ruled an 'error in navigation', with fortunately no loss of life.

As for the *River Clyde*, she managed to outlive all her human cargo's great names, eventually being scrapped in 1966 when, after long being under Spanish ownership, she was called *Marija y Aurora*.

Over the years, principally between the wars, there had been a number of attempts to reclaim her as some kind of public attraction – one report suggesting she could be moored in the Thames with people paying up to a shilling to look over her – but none actually succeeded.

She did, however, even under her new flag, share in one more moment of British-related endeavour, when she helped to rescue three downed British airmen during the Second World War.

> *Now to the old twilight and pale legendary glories,*
> *By our own youth outdone,*
> *Those shores recede; not there, but in memory everlasting*
> *The immortal heights were won.*
> *Of them that triumphed, of them that fell, there is only now*
> *Silence, and sleep, and fame,*
> *And in night's immensity far on that promontory's altar*
> *An invisibly burning flame.*
>
> Laurence Binyon, *Gallipoli*

Chapter 11

'Life's work well done'

I saw him before he won the VC; I saw him win it; I saw him wear
it. He was ever the same in the three stages. His death is universally
regretted and nowhere more so than in the Royal Navy. He is another
link with the grand and glorious past, gone from my life. He has left
behind him a shining example of all who go down to the sea in ships.

Dr Peter Burrowes Kelly

George's 'legacy', as it tends to be characterised these days, began to be forged even before he died. As if the widespread approbation for his deeds hadn't been celebrated enough at the time of his VC award, a year later, in 1917, they were further highlighted in an extraordinary, chest-thumping, tome, originally published by instalments, of pure, morale-boosting, propaganda unambiguously titled *Deeds that Thrill the Empire*.

To get the pulse racing even more, there was an even more hyperbolic subtitle, *'True Stories of the Most Glorious Acts of Heroism of the Empire's Soldiers and Sailors during the Great War'*. Two crammed volumes, no less, of black and white illustrations and colour plates, punctuating self-explanatory essays by 'well-known authors', intriguingly unidentified.

The tone is set from the start with a Foreword by Lord Derby, Secretary of State for War at the time, a man who'd done Army service in the Boer War and been mentioned twice in despatches, albeit in purely bureaucratic roles. He writes:

This book, containing records of brave deeds of our soldiers and sailors
in the present war, will not only bring pleasure to those whose near and

dear relatives have been engaged in such operations, but long after they have passed away will be an incentive to future generations to uphold the honour of our Flag. It is a worthy record of the fact that Britons, whether resident in the Mother Land, or in the Colonies, have not been unworthy of their brave predecessors.

The clue is in that first sentence: 'present war', and the whole unashamedly jingoistic, recruiting flavour of the document is further underscored in a long introduction which speaks of a nation *'threatened with a peril greater than the Napoleonic tyranny'*, and of *'self-deluded Teutons'* with their *'lust for world dominion'*.

'It is an epitaph,' it concludes, *'of those who have laid down their lives in setting so bright an example. It is a summons from those who remain to every fit man in the empire to go and do likewise.'* Lord Kitchener might have perished by the time of publication but his 'Your Country Needs You' rallying cry lived on.

In addition to a full-page colour plate of Charles Dixon's impression of the *River Clyde* landing at V Beach, there are a further three black and white illustrations of the action by war artist Edgar Holloway, including one very dramatic version of the landing with George, clearly in the foreground, head bandaged, helping to carry a wounded soldier to shore.

Then there's the essay itself – 'The *River Clyde*. How the Navy won six VCs in a day', which describes the operation – *'an exploit unparalleled in history'* – and the unfolding drama and heroism involving George, his fellow officers and seamen. *'No previous event had been signalized by the granting of so many Victoria Crosses; but no other in the history of the Cross had so well merited them,'* this 'well-known author' trumpeted.

Edgar Holloway worked prolifically for, among others, *The Boy's Own Paper*, which had been founded in 1879 to promote reading and strong Christian ethic. However, it was another artist, Algernon Black, who, in a copy of the popular paper, date unspecified, drew a spectacular version of the action depicting 'The VC Middies of the

Dardanelles', in which, with bullets raining in all around him and with the *River Clyde* in the background, George is seen swimming bravely from lighter to lighter with a rope.

Three years after P&O's Chairman, Lord Inchcape, had suggested to shareholders that George possessed just the right stuff to rise eventually to 'commodore', the so-called 'captain of captains', of the company fleet, he was reporting, just a month after the Armistice, the final toll of P&O dead during the war, totalling some 263. George, mentioned again in this despatch, was one of three group employees to be awarded the VC during the Great War.

Determined to maintain its standing as 'Postman to the World', P&O ships were inevitably in the line of fire. Fourteen company vessels were sunk by submarines while a further three succumbed to mines.

George's enduring link with the Imperial War Museum began with a letter dated 2 November 1918, exactly three months after his death and a day before what would have been his twenty-fourth birthday. It was also just a year or so on from the opening of the IWM (at the Crystal Palace in South London), and even more significantly, just nine days before the Armistice. George's father was writing to Major Charles ffoulkes, the first curator and secretary of the newly-founded museum, in response to what presumably was a plea for suitable materials to exhibit and archive.

'As requested in your notice in the papers,' Thomas Drewry wrote, 'I send you herewith a photo of my deceased son, copy of a letter from Dr Kelly RN DSO and a press cutting, together with the following summary of my son's service in the war …'

Ffoulkes replied three days later, in patriotic vein:

Dear Sir,
I am requested by the Committee of the Imperial War Museum to thank you very sincerely for sending us the photograph of your late son … together with the very interesting press cuttings about his wonderful career.

As to the photograph, it was naturally one of the first purchased by us to adorn our collection, so perhaps I better return it to you since very many would be glad to possess the portrait of such a famous young man.

The other details we shall be glad to keep in a separate section, and I will only add that, so long as the British Empire lasts, the name of your son will stand out as an exemplar to our Youth in letters of gold.

This swift and gracious response must have been of considerable succour to the still grieving family and especially to Thomas and Mary Ann. Thomas wrote back on 9 November:

Dear Sir,
I desire to thank you for the photo safely received and also for the very kind and generous letter which you sent.

Mrs Drewry and I are both very pleased and proud of your letter and it helps somewhat to console us for our great loss. Believe me, Sir.

Having experienced the almost indescribable sadness of outliving your child, Thomas Drewry, who worked as a naval architect in his later years, had the consolation, scant though it might have seemed, that he was survived by his wife and three other sons, who had all gone though the Great War comparatively unscathed. He died on 1 November 1925 aged 66 following an operation at the London (later Royal London) Hospital.

Like George, his funeral was at the City of London Cemetery on 4 November following a very well-attended service at All Saints Church, according to the *Stratford Express*. The local newspaper, noting his thirty-five years service with P&O, fourteen of them as assistant superintendent and works manager of the company's operation at Royal Albert Docks, also listed a host of other public roles which clearly marked out Thomas as a pillar of the community.

These included the Parochial Council, YMCA, All Saints Deaf and Dumb Mission, Forest Gate Ratepayers' Association, the Institute of Naval Architects, the Marine Engineers, and the Engineers and Ships' Affairs Association. Such diversity was reflected in the placing of no fewer than fifty floral wreaths at the graveside. Unsurprisingly, the paper also reported: *'It is interesting to recall that Mr Drewry was the father of the late Lieut George Leslie Drewry VC who so tragically met his death after the great honour had been conferred upon him ...'*

As well as his three surviving sons – the two oldest with their naval ranks still intact – recorded among the chief mourners that day, along with other members of the extended Drewry family, were also various representatives of P&O and the Docks department.

His name was then added to the impressive grave and headstone that already stood for George at the cemetery. To this memorial would later be added the names of Harry Kendall, Harry's wife Maud, and Mary Ann, who died in 1936 aged 75. 'Her children arise up and call her blessed her husband also and he praiseth her', was an inscribed dedication to this doughty mother of four.

Thomas left £17,000 in his will – equivalent to around £750,000 in today's terms – and he also bequeathed the following, deeply heartfelt, poem, *In Memoriam*, about George to his family.

> *So long as an English boy*
> *Shall read an English book*
> *So long as a tale is told*
> *By the fire or inglenook*
> *Your gallant brother's fame*
> *Will be talked about and read*
> *His memory and name*
> *Will live when we are dead*
>
> *Gentle and fearless was he*
> *The boy we gave*

Loving the Ships and the Sea
And restless wave

Braving the storm and fight
Torpedo and mine and shell
Battling for God and the right
Bravely and well

Guarding his Country's coast
So that we slept
Death found him there at his post
So faithfully kept.

Into thine Hands O Lord
Praying and weeping
We give the boy we loved
Into Thy keeping

Thousands of boys have we
Gentle and fearless
And of the battles they fought
Our island story
Shall tell of the dangers they sought
Shall tell of their glory

Oh! George my brother
Tis but a few years more
Then shall we greet each other
On yon distant shore

There side by side and hand in hand
We'll walk together day by day
In that dear land
Where God himself
Shall wipe all tears away.

Harry was the second Drewry son to die, in 1933, three years before his mother, aged 45. He had married Maud in 1927 but they had no children. They were living outside Manchester at Chorlton-cum-Hardy when he met his death just after Christmas while recuperating at Cliff House, Barton-on-Sea, Hampshire. The fact that his mother also died at Cliff House three years later, and that there are family letters from Percy in the 1940s on Cliff House-headed notepaper suggests that it had been another Drewry home for some time.

In poor health ever since the war, further exacerbated by the damp climate of the north-west, Harry's cause of death was given as 'haemoptysis caused by chronic pulmonary tuberculosis'. In layman's terms and as described to me by a medical professional: 'A dramatic and unpleasant departure. I only once witnessed a patient demise by coughing up blood (haemoptysis) a ghastly sight that still stays fresh in the mind. Pulmonary TB can be a chronic and invasive infection with rupture of the blood vessels a classic feature. Now, of course, rarely seen here because of immunization and anti-tubercular drugs.'

If George can be deemed to have achieved some kind of immortality through the award of his VC, then the Drewry family's most substantial earthly rewards were surely earned by Percy, who died in Wiltshire, at the age of 79.

We last met Percy when he was posted to Bordeaux in 1918 as a Naval transport officer. In the early 1920s, probably not long after he married his first wife, Stella, he set up his own business in France as a merchant in the shipping and coal trade, becoming eventually the biggest supplier in France of coal to, among other industries, the French railways and steel works.

After carefully monitoring the emergence of the oil industry, Percy switched his activities from coal to oil in the early 1930s and by the outbreak of the Second World War was operating from Paris a fleet of some fifty tankers – about thirty on his charter and a further twenty as a broker.

Rumoured at that time to be the biggest tanker operator in the world, he was also a pioneer of tanker freight contracts in markets spanning the Persian Gulf to Europe and California to Japan, as well as opening up many trades and several world record sized cargoes. By 1939 he was shifting oil for companies in many parts of the world, such as the Persian Gulf, Eastern Mediterranean and the Black Sea, California, the US Gulf, Ecuador and Peru.

Only the outbreak of war apparently stopped him becoming a ship owner, as at the time he was negotiating the purchase of at least two 16,000 tonne tankers to employ in his freight contracts.

In 1940 he left Paris less than twenty-four hours before the Germans marched in, and for a short time after that he assisted the French oil industry in its reorganization, for which he was awarded the *Medaille de Reconnaissance*.

When France fell, he left the country at the very last moment with his second wife, Isobel Jessie, twenty-two years his junior, after a very tortuous journey. This included just missing being on board the RMS *Lancastria* when she was sunk off St Nazaire (evacuating British nationals and troops two weeks after Dunkirk with the loss of more than 4,000 lives), driving through the advancing German columns towards a trawler just as the port was about to be taken and having the trawler next to them sunk.

Landing again on the Spanish frontier, going through Spain and Portugal, and finally being chased by a German submarine in a vessel disguised as a fishing smack on the way from Portugal, they finally reached the UK.

It was just as well he didn't fall into the hands of the Germans as just prior to the outbreak of war he had diverted and retarded many oil cargoes to Germany, which were vitally needed for the enemy war effort.

During the war he acted as an adviser to the British Government on oil and shipping matters, particularly in connection with France where he had lived and worked for some twenty years.

Percy found time to be with the ARP in London throughout the Blitz and in the Home Guard. As an ex-Navy man he was able to join the Navy Small Vessels pool ferrying small craft down to the South Coast in preparation for the D-Day landings, as well as taking part in subsequent landings.

Soon after returning to the UK he and Isobel bought Rainscombe Park, a beautiful Wiltshire estate near Pewsey in over 450 acres, complete with a large, Grade II listed, two-storey mansion built in the early part of the nineteenth century. They also acquired a Rolls-Royce and hosted the local hunt.

In memory of George – after whom Percy named his only child (by Stella) – he set up scholarships for the sons of Merchant Navy officers and seamen who had died as a result of war action, and later took an interest in the Southampton School of Navigation.

In 1945 he returned to Paris to find his pre-war business, which had ceased with the Occupation, completely broken up and effectively non-existent. Despite very poor health in the years after the war, Percy returned repeatedly to Paris to try, successfully as it turned out, to restart his shipping consultancy business despite very difficult conditions.

By the 1950s he turned his focus more and more to the UK, his particular concern being the decline of the British Merchant Navy fleet in the face of the rise of fleets under the tax-free flags of convenience. In this connection he was in close touch with the Merchant Officers Federation, the National Union of Seamen and the different government departments and committees on a non-party basis, which he believed to be of great national importance.

Despite, or perhaps because of, his declining health, he and Isobel travelled all over the world regularly by ship over the next twenty years; to Buenos Aires on RMS *Highland Princess*; to Wellington, New Zealand on RMS *Rangitoto*; to the west coast of South America on the SS *Reina Del Mar* and to Cape Town, South Africa on the RMS *Pendennis Castle*. Percy's listed occupation on those various ships' manifests spanned 'Shipping Manager' to 'Landowner', betraying his rise and rise from salaried man to multi-millionaire. He was recalled by members of the family as 'good, generous and worldly'.

The ship broking business continued in Paris under his son George who, a year after Percy's death in 1969, then funded a new UK company, HP Drewry, specialising in shipping research.

The name eventually changed to Drewry Shipping Consultants and, although there was a management buy-out in 2000 followed a few months later by George's death, the company still operates under that name to this day. The connection between the name Drewry and the sea lives on.

As for Ralph, just out of his teens at war's end, he also had his fair share of near terminal scrapes during a fifty-year career as a boilermaker/plater. Once, while working on the liner *Jervis Bay* (later to become an armoured convoy escort before being sunk by the pocket battleship *Admiral Scheer* in 1940), he fell into a coal bunker and suffered a locked jaw.

Later, as he recalled in his decidedly doleful memoir, there was an occasion when, horrified, he witnessed a huge crane on the quay topple and crash down on a ship, killing two dockers. He was then ordered to supervise the burning of the crane in two halves to try and make it easier for a floating crane to lift the pieces off – 'all night in pouring rain, a terrible job. I was nearly knocked out by hoisting cable.'

In 1937, now married to Emily, who was born deaf, and the father of two sons, George and Ralph, he went to work for Stratford, East London-based Towler and Son, manufacturers of steel fabricated platework, where he remained for the next twenty-three years until his retirement. During the war, and throughout the Blitz and beyond, Towler's was much involved in defence work as well as the construction of invasion barges.

Surviving serious bombing raids at least six times while at work, Ralph got to play hero again when he was on the scene after a fellow worker stepped on a high voltage welding cable inside an 8ft cylinder tank and was so shocked he couldn't move.

'I had no time to think,' wrote Ralph, 'so without hesitation I put my arms around the man and pulled him out through a sixteen-inch hole. What surprised me was that I was unharmed and the next day the poor man had recovered. The Works Manager congratulated me for saving him from being electrocuted.'

Throughout his long and often difficult life, much of it at a time when deafness was a much-misunderstood disability, Ralph's hero sibling was never far from his thoughts.

In *A Place Called Armageddon*, centred around a series of letters from the Great War, Michael Moynihan wrote, in a chapter about George, 'he [Ralph] still talks with emotion of the brother who was his only close companion in childhood and whose death he has never ceased to mourn ... On the sideboard there is a framed photograph of George among those of his two sons and two grandchildren and a copy of the oil painting he made of the *River Clyde*, now on permanent display at Merchant Taylor's School.'

Inspired by the famous painting of the *River Clyde* at V Beach by Charles Dixon, Ralph's version, dated 1927, adorns the cover of this book.

Ralph, widowed in 1970, outlasted all his brothers and died in 1987 at Worthing aged 89, just twenty-five miles along the Sussex coast from where his surviving son, George, in his eighty-ninth year, now lives.

As well as Ralph's painting, his brother's old school also boasts the *River Clyde* ship's bell, its copper housing still gleaming, and the original family album of slightly fraying press cuttings about George's VC action. Also there on the school's war memorial board, studded with Remembrance Day poppies for the entire Great War centenary, is George's name inscribed modestly between 'Donald B.S.' and 'Dudley E.W.'. Some stirring lines from Edmund Spenser's epic sixteenth century poem, 'The Fairie Queene', are carved above the roll-call of the school's fallen: 'Nought is more honorable to a knight then to defend the feeble in their right.'

Merchant Taylors', which had moved from the Charterhouse to the more rural setting of Northwood, Middlesex in 1933, was also the backdrop when, in December 1966, Percy presented the school with five new swimming trophies in memory of George. Then in 1996, several members of the Drewry clan, including Ralph's George and Percy's George – the cousins hadn't met in nearly thirty years – along with representatives of the Victoria Cross and George Cross Association and a pair of Gallipoli veterans foregathered at Northwood. The occasion was the handing over of George's VC – which had been in the care of the school since 1918 – to the Imperial War Museum for permanent display alongside, at the time, forty other VC and George crosses.

The medal was presented by the school's senior naval cadet to the IWM's chairman, Lord Bramall, who said: 'The Victoria Cross is the most distinguished award, taking precedence over all other orders, medals and decorations. It can involve making the ultimate sacrifice for your country and Lieutenant Drewry displayed a truly herculean effort at Gallipoli in 1915. We must never allow ourselves to forget this important event in history and by allowing the museum to put the medal on show it will act as a constant reminder to us all.'

Today, George's medal features among the world's largest collection of VCs in the IWM's Lord Ashcroft Gallery, which was opened by HRH The Princess Royal in 2010. The exhibit, which includes interactive touch-screens, video montage, and sound clips, is called, appropriately, 'Extraordinary Heroes'.

Another 'reminder' had arrived at the Museum back in 1938 with the unveiling, in April of that year, of a magnificently detailed diorama, a large three-dimensional model, more than 6ft across by almost 4ft in depth, of the V Beach landing. It was the work of prolific London-born, painter and modelmaker Dennis 'Denny' Stokes whose involvement in other similar presentations ranged from the Romans landing in Britain in 55BC to D-Day 1944.

His Gallipoli model depicts the *River Clyde* aground some 300ft from the shore, with Royal Munster Fusiliers pouring down its gangways attempting to land by means of three lighters. George's hopper *Argyle* is also there, shown in the centre of the diorama, grounded in such a position as to be useless as part of the improvised pontoon from ship to shore. On the extreme right is the old fort of Sedd-el-Bahr.

Among some 250 figures are Unwin and Seaman Williams, which were added following an exchange of correspondence between Stokes, who funded the project himself, the IWM and Unwin. Closer inspection of the hopper suggests that both 'Geordie' Samson and George are also represented; perhaps an early example of what are commonly referred to today as 'action figures'.

Although the IWM, sadly, didn't take up further offers by Stokes to create other First World War tableaux, his Gallipoli model remained on show for more than sixty years until 2012. It now resides in store at the IWM's Duxford facility.

Interestingly, the Turks have their own version, albeit a considerable cruder and less detailed diorama of the action, which is on permanent view at the otherwise impressive Military Marine Museum at Canakkale.

The events at V Beach and of George's short life would continue to reverberate down the years in other arenas, too.

A year after the Western Front was immortalized for the first time on sound film in a Hollywood produced, Anglo-American adaptation of R.C. Sherriff's hugely successful 1928 stage play, *Journey's End*, Gallipoli got the movie treatment in 1931's *Tell England*. Although its script, from Ernest Raymond's novel, wasn't nearly as sharp and perceptive as *Journey's End*, it easily trumped the earlier film with some startling action sequences, notably a ten-minute or so, virtually dialogue-free, brutally realistic, recreation of the V Beach landing which even included stunt doubles for the *River Clyde*, Unwin and Williams.

In fact, so authentic-looking was this action footage in stark monochrome that it would be utilized regularly down the years in many subsequent documentaries, Turkish-produced among them, about the Dardanelles campaign.

Tell England was co-directed by Anthony 'Puffin' Asquith and Geoffrey Barkas, a tandem extraordinarily well-suited to such a project. Asquith – who'd later become best known for his film work with writer Terence Rattigan – was, after all, the son of Herbert Asquith, Prime Minister at the time of the April landings, while Barkas was a Suvla Bay veteran. He would become a pioneer of twentieth century military camouflage and enemy deception, which probably helps to explain the credibility of lookalike locations on Malta. The filmmakers also credited the co-operation of the Admiralty, which arranged for warships of the Mediterranean squadron to be put at their disposal.

In the early 1950s came news that the Admiralty had decided to do without midshipmen in the fleet altogether (eventually implemented in 1957) so breaking with naval tradition going back to the first Elizabethan era or earlier. This was a perfect excuse to recall a glorious tradition, typified in an article by Captain R. Barry O'Brien in the *Portsmouth Evening News* of 29 June 1954, which suggested, as he delved into the archives of individual achievement, that the very term 'midshipman' was somehow synonymous with bravery.

He wrote: '*Times without number they distinguished themselves, just as they did … during the Gallipoli landings, where they ran the picket boats, earning the greatest admiration of both British and Australian troops in the process.*' He recalled, in particular, George and Wilfred Malleson as well as other, VC-winning, young midshipmen from mid-nineteenth century actions such as Inkerman in the Crimea, the Indian Mutiny and, more obscurely, the attack on the Shimonoseki Forts, Japan, in 1863–4.

Almost a century after George's life was commemorated with the memorial window at his church, he received another local accolade on the centenary of his deeds when a specially inscribed stone in his name was laid at the Cenotaph in Central Park, East Ham, less than two miles from the old family home.

More than 200 gathered at the morning ceremony on 27 April 2015, at which Sir Robin Wales, Mayor of Newham Council, that organized the event as part of an ongoing initiative to recognize other VC winners from the borough during the Great War, said: 'It is right that we remember people who have died serving their country. Though they did extraordinary things, they were ordinary people like all of us. We have unveiled this commemorative stone to salute George's devotion to duty under fire and it will serve as a lasting monument to his valour. The actions he took in Gallipoli are an example of selflessness and bravery to which we can aspire.'

'Gallipoli hero' is this biography's subtitle. The very term 'hero' is, in today's parlance, so often instantly and indiscriminately applied, and as frequently misused, that it has for many, become essentially devalued. Maybe some more distance is required to judge its essence.

'Show me a hero and I will write you a tragedy', opined F. Scott Fitzgerald. 'The hero is strangely akin to those who die young', suggested the Austrian poet Rilke who, like the American, was called up for service in the Great War but remained a safe distance from the front line.

George's short, accident-prone, life perfectly illuminates elements of both observations. However, judged from the distance of more than a century, his heroism among the heroism of so many others less recognised in that terrible war, still remains both authentic and a beacon.

This book began with an extract from the *Melbourne Argus*, written in 1937. Almost thirty years on, in November 1966, D.C. Thomson's *The Hornet*, a British boys' comic, also immortalized George in a front and back page colour strip headlined 'Boy Overboard!' which recreated scenes, not from Gallipoli but instead, rather surprisingly, from his mishaps aboard the *Indian Empire*.

The account ended, however, with a complimentary reference to his later deeds at the Dardanelles, declaring 'George Drewry was certainly a lad with guts.'

That sentiment could possibly have served as some sort of epitaph. The official version on George's headstone, proclaims, however, a rather less emotive single line: simply and straightforwardly, 'Life's work well done'.

There it was: of scimitar shape with its mouldered fortress on this nearer headland and the tall cape beyond – the cape, which gave its grand terrible name to all. There was the low bank of sand with the drowsy ripples slinking up towards it in their sleep. That tiny cliff of sand! But how quiet it all was. Surely if one listened one must hear ghostly reverberations, surely a swarm of grey phantoms should sweep over sand and hills. But no: it lay there facing the calm blue sea like some Cornish beach after the summer visitors have gone.

Ernest Raymond, *The Quiet Shore*

Stories from Real Life: *Melbourne Argus*, 28 April 1937

'I have been ordered to report for active service, sir', said George Drewry, as he stepped into his commander's cabin on the P&O liner at Port Said.

'Well, goodbye my boy,' said the commander gripping the young officer's hand warmly: 'you will keep the old flag flying?' He was sorry to part with the modest lad who was so competent for his 18 years.

'I will do my best, sir,' said young Drewry.

Arrangements had been made for George to join HMS *Hussar* at Alexandria. He wasted no time getting there. 'HMS *Hussar* pinnace, sir?' inquired a smart blue-jacket, saluting the new midshipman and soon they were chugging across the harbor at Alexandria to where the *Hussar* lay at anchor. The great adventure had begun.

But stern days were ahead. George little dreamt he would be taking part in the landing at Gallipoli a few months later. The fleet was to co-operate with the Expeditionary Force and help in covering the landing of the troops with its fire.

On the evening of April 23 1915, the *River Clyde*, an old collier which had been specially prepared for landing operations, started on her perilous mission with other British transports to the Dardanelles. Towing three lighters on her port side and with a steam barge on her starboard, she crept towards the peninsula. There was a feeling of suppressed excitement on board as they anchored for the night.

'This is bad luck,' remarked the commander at daybreak, for the weather had changed and a strong wind and a rough sea made it doubtful whether the expedition would be managed successfully.

However, the weather became calmer and about four o'clock in the afternoon 2,000 British troops were brought alongside and transferred to the *River Clyde*.

'Proceed at midnight!' came the command.

'It looks peaceful enough so far,' said one of the lads to his mate.

'We'll hear something before long, I fancy,' was the reply, 'this looks like business!'

'Take your bearings from the Turkish searchlights, quartermaster,' said Commander Unwin as the vessel steered slowly against the current. 'Look out, ahoy!' shouted the office on the forecastle. 'Keep your eyes wide open for any sign of mines or periscopes.' He was thinking of the soldiers crowded in the holds.

At daybreak on Sunday April 25, Midshipman Drewry was ordered to take charge of the steam barge which was being towed. Then, leaving the covering squadron, they headed for the dim outline of the most southern portion of the peninsula near Cape Helles. At Anzac Cove, further north the Australians had already begun their share in the great assault on Gallipoli.

'We're getting too far east,' thought the commander anxiously, as the vessels began to shear slightly out of their course. There must be no hitch.

'"Lizzie" is showing her teeth,' said a blue-jacket as the *Queen Elizabeth* began to bombard the shore, 'can't she growl!' Battleships, cruisers, and destroyers blazed away, and the land seemed to be a mass of fire and smoke. Not a gun was fired in reply. The beach was strongly defended, and the enemy having been well warned, had yet another trench halfway up the cliff. It was so quiet that it seemed as if the troops might have a chance to land without opposition.

So now it was a race to get the soldiers safely ashore. But within half a mile of the beach they had orders to wait. Then at last the signal was given and the *River Clyde* dashed forward and ran aground as arranged close to the shore. The steam barge, with young Drewry in charge, went ahead and grounded on the port bow. At the same instant a torrent of fire broke out from the shore. Shot spattered the *River Clyde* like hailstones.

'What did I tell you?' asked a soldier of his mate.

'It's hot enough now, anyway!'

The idea had been to make a bridge of lighters to the beach so that the 2,000 soldiers could emerge through the openings that had been cut in the side of the *River Clyde*, drop to the lighters and rush ashore without hindrance. But the unexpected happened.

'The lighters have broken adrift!' exclaimed Commander Unwin in dismay. Under terrific fire from the enemy, men began to pour out on to the incomplete bridge, which it was impossible to cross!

What could be done? The lighters had failed to reach their proper positions, and the commander was risking his life in an heroic effort to keep them together.

'I'll take a line ashore, sir,' volunteered Midshipman Drewry and jumping over the bow of the steam barge he waded towards a reef to make a line fast. He was a target for snipers and the bullets fell in a shower about him, but he took no heed. Meeting a soldier desperately wounded in the water, Drewry tried to carry him ashore. The next minute the poor fellow was killed in the middy's arms.

Throwing away his revolver, coat and hat, Drewry raced along the beach, and wading into the water again, pulled with all his might to try and get the lighters into position and close up the gap in that shot-swept bridge. Going to the help of his commander, who was also in the water battling with the lighters, the intrepid lad volunteered to go back for more rope.

The shower of shrapnel continued. Tirelessly the young midshipman struggled to keep the lighters in position so that the troops might have the best chance. One moment he would be in the water wading or swimming with a line, the next he would be on a lighter fixing it.

'You're hit, lad!' A lieutenant on the lighter saw young Drewry fall as a piece of shrapnel struck him, wounding him in the head. Stunned and bleeding he lay on the drifting lighter. But his work was not finished.

'Bind it up with that,' he begged, pointing to a soldier's scarf. Then, in spite of his wounds, he managed to make the lighter fast. He watched incessantly to see where help was most urgently wanted.

'Another rope needed!' In a moment, Drewry had jumped overboard and was swimming with a line between his teeth to complete his difficult and dangerous task. And now a shot severed the lashing rope, and the lighters were adrift again!

But Drewry never thought of giving in. Off with a line once more, under heavy rifle and machine-gun fire! But his strength was failing. Just one last effort – the knot – he must fix it. Then Midshipman Drewry knew no more. They carried him aboard the *River Clyde*, exhausted and delirious.

Living with the Legacy

George Thomas Drewry, oldest surviving nephew, and his daughter, acclaimed artist Skye Holland, reflect personally on their distinguished relative's legacy:

George: Sometime after my parents moved from Forest Gate to Loughton on the edge of the Epping Forest when I was five years old, I first became aware of a large studio portrait in sepia of George L. Drewry.

He was in full naval uniform adorned by his VC ribbon, seated on a Victorian-framed studio seat with bowed armrests with his left hand resting on the hilt of his Sword of Honour standing upright beside his left leg.

This portrait occupied much of the wall at the top of the staircase and, in this commanding position, could be seen by visitors whenever the front door was fully opened. My proud father [*Ralph Drewry*] greeted first time visitors by drawing their attention up the staircase towards the portrait, simply saying 'My brother, VC'.

Opposite the portrait, hanging on the bulkhead above the stairs, was a replica of my father's large oil painting of the *River Clyde* landing troops at V Beach in the face of intense Turkish gunfire from the high ground overlooking the beach. When my brother and I, then aged 6 and 8 respectively, were sent to a small boarding school for deaf boys at Northampton, we were reunited with the portrait and painting during our school holidays. But it was the Sword of Honour that we hunted for and found hidden in a wardrobe. The inscription on the inside of the sword hand guard filled us with awe as we realized our heroic uncle was the first officer of the RNR and the Merchant Service to be awarded the VC.

We also came across a book *Gallipoli* by John Masefield, which was presented to our uncle by the Lady Mayoress of Liverpool. Naturally, as boys would do, we play-acted with the sword and a First World War Belgian bayonet.

It was not until I was about seventeen that I uncovered a small collection of press cuttings recording my uncle's deeds at V Beach and his later untimely accidental death and started to understand more about the Gallipoli campaign.

In my conversations with my father, I detected an undertone of his lifelong lament over the loss of his brother and close childhood friend and felt that in the poem written after my uncle's death by my grandfather, Thomas Drewry, he showed an insight into this close relationship.

I recall my father getting excited when he was invited to attend the opening of the VC Centenary Exhibition at Marlborough House in 1956. On his return he showed me a brochure marking this event and described how he located his brother's VC medal with its blue ribbon in one of the rooms. He was full of pride but, on reflection years later, I felt he did not get the full benefit of the occasion as he was deaf and would, if this event had taken place in more recent years, have benefited from the services of a sign language interpreter like many deaf people do when they, for example, go to hospital appointments or attend public meetings.

In subsequent years, I visited the Imperial War Museum and saw a new tableau of the *River Clyde* at V Beach in a special exhibition and followed up several years later with a visit to Nigel Steel of the museum's Department of Documents, who showed me the Sword of Honour and George's letters home. I identified the sword as the one I had grown up with.

It was a relief to see it again in a good place as it had gone astray during house clearance following my father's death; it had, by good fortune, been spotted and snapped up by the IWM at an auction in Lewes, Sussex.

Nigel Steel kindly gave me a copy of his article describing the *River Clyde*'s operation at V Beach as akin to the 'Wooden Horse at Troy'. This aroused my interest even more.

It was only in the last ten to fifteen years that, with my son, Hamish, living in Cambridge with his wife and children, my wife, Roba and I accompanied them to visit the famous orchard at Grantchester and have tea under the spreading branches of the apple trees.

Here, where Rupert Brooke and the rest of the Bloomsbury Group used to meet, we visited a wooden hut next to the servery that housed some documents and booklets relating to the Gallipoli campaign.

On one occasion we came across the father-in-law of my son's old school friend who told us of his life-long interest in the history of the Gallipoli campaign and my uncle's part in it and of his frequent visits to the Gallipoli peninsula to show some people over the landing beaches and Turkish trenches on high ground overlooking same.

Since then, I have read *Birds Without Wings* by Louis de Bernières, which, in part, described the Gallipoli campaign from the Turkish standpoint. By this time, I had acquired a deeper understanding of what the Gallipoli campaign involved, and my uncle's part in it – through osmosis, as my daughter, Skye, puts it.

Indeed, when I recently examined an enlargement of a small photograph of my uncle leaning over the side of his new ship (HMT *William Jackson*, of which he had taken command to go patrolling in Northern Waters shortly before his accidental death), and studied his (in Skye's words) 'gentle and insistent gaze', I felt a spiritual connection that bridged almost a hundred years.

It infused me with a sense of kinship accompanied by a glow of quiet pride.

Skye: From quite an early age, I have memories of visiting my grandad's bungalow in Worthing and seeing the VC and Sword of

Honour hanging on the wall behind the dining table. I also remember being shown various pictures of him, the reproduction copy of my grandad's painting of the *River Clyde* and photos of the heroic brother.

To be perfectly honest, this was as interesting to me as a child as what was in the garden to play with, like squashing the red ants on the coal bunker cover with my brother, and other childhood games to while away the long afternoons!

As an adult, while decorating my home, I chose to create a family gallery of sepia and black and white framed photos. In that gallery, there's a beautiful and rather ethereal photo of the enigmatic and youthful Royal Navy-clad Great Uncle George. He had a gentle and insistent gaze, which was fascinating to me.

So his presence in my life had been secured, and my children have grown up seeing that portrait and knowing that he is part of their family legacy and DNA. An acceptance by visual osmosis, if you like!

It was only when my 25-year old son Lucien made the slightly shocking decision to move to Sydney, Australia and find a job that (I had been a single parent for many years by this time) his sister Emmanuelle, my parents Roba and George, Lucien and I decided to trip off to the Imperial War Museum and give Great Uncle George a visit.

Why? Perhaps it was the need to reinforce family bonds, create a sense of belonging. Those were probably my motivations, as well as a good thing to do on a day out with grandma and grandpa before he left.

The Imperial War Museum had been refurbished and we moved swiftly towards the newly interactive VC room – where George had pride of place in a gallery of other heroes. I was fascinated to watch my two grown-up children pressing the buttons – moving images back and forth, reading letters, studying the VC itself.

The old family rhetoric about him became much more real and alive. George's heroism and the horrors of Gallipoli, and the First World War (which Lucien had studied at university) became newly poignant.

The sword is no longer an ornament, rather a symbol of honour and bravery. We left the building with a new sense of connection to this family member, and a great deal of real pride.

I recently saw the movie *Dunkirk* and was reminded of the terrible losses women endured in war – husbands, sons, fathers and brothers.

Despite Lucien being 15,000 miles away in Australia, he has grown up living in peacetime, as safe and secure as any of us can hope to be living in a modern world with a different brand of threat.

I drew courage from that and realised that whatever problems we think we have, however much separation and the sense of loss I feel at my children leaving home and being so far away, I am blessed. They are blessed. I carry that kernel of pride deep within.

So I owe it to my Great Uncle George for being who he was in such difficult times. If his portrait could talk, I'd say 'hello! and 'Thank you!' out loud, and long for a reply.

Sources/Bibliography

Arthur, Max, *Forgotten Voices of the Great War*, Ebury Press, 2002

Ashmead-Bartlett, E., *Uncensored Dardanelles*, Hutchinson & Co, 1928

Aspinall-Oglander, Brigadier-General C.F., *Military Operations Gallipoli, Vol 1 & 2*, William Heinemann, 1929-1932

Baldwin, Hanson, *World War 1: An Outline History*, Hutchinson, 1963

Best, Kenneth, *War Diaries: A Chaplain at Gallipoli, edited by Gavin Roynon* Simon & Schuster, 2011

Billington, Rachel, *Glory: A Story of Gallipoli*, Orion, 2015

Binyon, Laurence, *extract from 'Gallipoli'*, 1915

Broadbent, Harvey, *Defending Gallipoli*, Melbourne University Press, 2015

Bush, Eric, *Gallipoli*, Allen & Unwin, 1975

Carlyon, L.A., *Gallipoli*, Bantam, 2003

Cavell, Samantha, *A Social History of Midshipmen and Quarterdeck Boys in the Royal Navy 1796-1831*, Exeter University, 2010

Chasseaud, Peter, *Mapping the First World War*, Imperial War Museum, 2013

Chasseaud, Peter and Doyle, Peter, *Grasping Gallipoli*, Spellmount, 2005

Churchill Winston, *The Great War, Part Work Vols 10,11, 12 & 13*, George Newnes, 1933

Cohen, M.J. *The Penguin Thesaurus of Quotations*, Penguin, 1998

De Bernières, Louis, *Birds Without Wings*, Secker & Warburg, 2004

Dearmer, Geoffrey, *extract from poem to his late brother*, 1918

Deeds that Thrill the Empire, N&M Press reprint of 1917 original

Denham, H.M., *Dardanelles: A Midshipman's Diary*, John Murray, 1981

Doyle, Peter, *Battle Story: Gallipoli 1915*, Spellmount, 2011

Drewry, George Leslie VC, *Letters to his father: 12 May, 25 September, 7 October, 12 November, 1915*, IWM

Englund, Peter, *The Beauty and the Sorrow: An Intimate History of the First World War*, Profile, 2012

Erickson, Edward J., *Gallipoli: The Ottoman Campaign*, Pen & Sword Military, 2010

Fleming, Colin, *Novel Helmsmen*, The Smart Set, 2016

Forester, C.S., *Mr Midshipman Hornblower*, Little, Brown & Company, 1948

Fussell, Paul, *The Great War and Modern Memory*, Oxford University Press, 2000

Draper, F.W.M., *Four Centuries of Merchant Taylors' School 1561-1961*, Oxford University Press, 1962

Gilbert, Martin, *The First World War*, HarperCollins, 1995

Great War, The ... I Was There! Undying memories of 1914-1918 issue 8, edited by Sir J. Hammerton, part work 1938-1939

Hamilton, Sir Ian, *First Gallipoli Despatch, 6 July 1915*, London Gazette

Hamilton, Sir Ian, *Third Gallipoli Despatch, 6 January 1916*, London Gazette

Hamilton, Sir Ian, *Gallipoli Diary Vol I & II*, Edward Arnold, 1920

Hargrave, John, *The Suvla Bay Landing*, Macdonald, 1964

Harris, Clive, *interview*, 21 March, 2017

Hart, Peter, *Gallipoli*, Profile, 2013

Hart, Peter, *Military History Monthly: Issue 9*, 2015

Herbert, A.P., *The Secret Battle*, Methuen, 1919

Kannengeiser, Hans, *The Campaign In Gallipoli*, Hutchinson, 1927

Keegan. John. *The First World War*, Hutchinson, 1998

Kent, Alexander, *Midshipman Bolitho*, Hutchinson, 1975

Keyes, Admiral Sir Roger, *The Fight for Gallipoli*, Eyre & Spottiswoode, 1941

Konstam, Angus, *Scapa Flow*, Osprey, 2009

Liddell Hart, B.H., *Liddell Hart's History of The First World War*, Cassell & Co, 1934

Liddle, Peter, *Men of Gallipoli*, David & Charles, 1976

Mackenzie, Compton, *Gallipoli Memories*, Cassell, 1929

Marryat, Frederick, *Mr Midshipman Easy*, Macmillan, 1836

Masefield, John, *Gallipoli*, Heinemann, 1916

Mayes, Gilbert and Thompson, Michael, *Cochrane Shipbuilders: Vol 2: 1915-1939*, Bernard McCall, 2014

Merchant Taylors' School, Oxford, Basil Blackwell, 1929

Moorehead, Alan, *Gallipoli*, First Four Square, 1963

Moynihan, Michael, *People at War*, David & Charles, 1973

Moynihan, Michael, *A Place Called Armageddon: Letters from The Great War*, David & Charles, 1975

Mure, Major A.H., *With the Incomparable 29th*, W&R Chambers, 1919

Murray, Joseph, *Gallipoli 1915*, Silvertail, 2015

O'Brian, Patrick, *Master & Commander*, HarperCollins, 1970

Paxman, Jeremy, *Great Britain's Great War*, Penguin/Viking, 2013

Raymond, Ernest, *Tell England: A Study in a Generation*, Cassell & Co, 1922

Raymond, Ernest, *The Quiet Shore*, Cassells, 1958

Reeman, Douglas, *HMS Saracen*, Arrow, 2003

Reeman, Douglas, *The Horizon, Arrow*, 2006

Robson, Stephen and O'Donoghue, Kevin, *P&O: A Fleet History*, World Ship Society, 1988

Samson, Air Commodore Charles, *Fights and Flights*, Ernest Benn, 1930

Sandford, Christopher, *The Final Over: The Cricketers of Summer 1914* Spellmount, 2014

Sassoon, Siegfried, *extract from 'To My Brother'*, 1918

Shaw-Stewart, Patrick, *extract from 'I Saw a Man this Morning'*, 1915

Snelling, Stephen, *Gallipoli: VCs of the First World War*, The History Press, 2010

Snelling, Stephen, *The Wooden Horse of Gallipoli*, Frontline, 2017

Steel, Nigel, *Gallipoli*, Pen & Sword, 1999

Steel, Nigel, *The Landing at Helles: V Beach* (unpublished chapter) and *V Beach and the River Clyde: The Epitome of Gallipoli* (unpublished chapter), 1993

The Times History of the War Vols V, VI & VII

Unwin, Captain Edward VC, *The Landing from the River Clyde* (from his private papers), Imperial War Museum

Van Emden, Richard and Chambers, Stephen, *Gallipoli: The Dardanelles Disaster in Soldiers' Words and Photographs*, Bloomsbury, 2015

Wedgwood, Lieutenant Commander Josiah, MP DSO, *Letter to Churchill, 25 April, 1915*, Unwin Private Papers, Imperial War Museum

Wedgwood, Lieutenant Commander Josiah, MP, DSO, *With Machine Guns in Gallipoli*, Darling & Son, 1915

Weld Forester, Wolstan Beaumont Charles, *From Dartmouth to the Dardanelles*, The Echo Library, 2015

Weldon, Captain L.W., *Hard Lying: Eastern Mediterranean 1914-1919*, Herbert Jenkins, 1925

Wester-Wemyss, Lord, *The Navy in the Dardanelles Campaign*, Hodder & Stoughton, 1924

Wilkinson, Norman, *The Dardanelles*, Longmans/Green & Co, 1915

Wilson, Ben, *Empire of the Deep: The Rise and Fall of the British Navy*, Weidenfeld & Nicolson, 2013

Index

A Beach, 77, 81, 83, 88, 97–8
All Saints Church, Forest Gate, 123,
  130
Anafarta, 80, 91
Anzac Cove, *ix*, *xii*, 77, 79–80, 82, 89,
  91–2, 95–6, 144
Argyle (hopper), 2, 8, 34, 38–9, 139
Ari Burnu, 90–1
Arthur, Max, 101
Ashmead-Bartlett, Ellis, *xiii*, 53, 76
Aspinall-Oglander, Brig Gen, 8, 103
Asquith, Anthony, 140
Asquith, Herbert, 56, 140

B Beach, 77, 81, 83, 86
Barkas, Geoffrey, 140
Beatty, V Adml Sir David, 106, 108
Beresford, Lord Charles, 117
Bernières, Louis de, *xv*, 104, 149
Billington, Rachel, *xv*, 41
Binyon, Laurence, *xv*, 126
Birds Without Wings (book), 104, 149
Black, Algernon, 128
Boer War, 5, 13, 41, 127
Boxer Rebellion, 5, 41
Boy's Own Paper, The (newspaper),
  128
Bramall, Lord, 138
Brooke, Rupert, xv, 149
Brooks, Ernest, 64
Brown Brothers, 106
Buck and Hickman Limited, 111
Buckingham Palace, 72–3
Bulletin, The (magazine), 63

Bush, Capt Eric, 117
Byng, Lt Gen (later FM) Julian, 94,
  100

C Beach, 77, 81, 83, 86–7
Cavell, Dr Samantha, 19, 21
Canakkale, *x*, *xiii*, *xix*, 10, 77, 82, 139
Cape Helles, *xi–xii*, *xv*, 2–3, 8, 10, 34,
  65, 77, 79, 82, 144
Cape Horn, 29
Carington-Smith, Lt Col Herbert, 45
Carlyon, L.B. 'Les', 6
Carpenters' Company Institute,
  14–15
Chambers, Stephen, *xvii*, 89, 93
Charterhouse, The, 15
Chocolate Hill, 80
Christian, R Adml Charles Arbuthnot,
  86
Churchill, Winston, *xiii*, 1, 25, 48, 56,
  99, 103, 124
City of London Cemetery, 124, 130
Claremont Road, 58 (*aka*
  'Welholme'), 13, 18
Cleethorpes, 11
Cochrane and Sons, 117
Cornwell, Jack, 109
Costeker, Capt John, 45
Cowan, Capt Walter, 107
Crookenden, Capt Arthur, 92–3

Daily Express (newspaper), 58, 60
Daily Mirror (newspaper), 64
Daily Sketch (newspaper), 58

Daily Telegraph (newspaper), 57
Dardanelles, *viii*, x, xiii, xvii, 2–4, 18,
    43, 52, 55, 58–9, 62–3, 73, 93, 99,
    103, 125, 141, 143
Dardanelles: A Midshipmen's Diary
    (book), 24
Dartmouth, 23–4
Dearmer, Geoffrey, *xv*, 95
Deeds that Thrill the Empire
    (magazine), 127–8
Denham, H.M., 24–5
Derby, 17th Earl of, 127
Derry Journal (newspaper), 31
Devonport, 24, 77, 111
Dixon, Charles, 128, 137
Dogger Bank, Battle of, 106
Doughty-Wylie VC, Lt Col Charles
    'Dick', 5, 46, 64
Doyle, Peter, *xvii*, 53–4, 78, 100
Draper, F.W.M., 15
Drewry VC, George Leslie, *xi*,
    xiii–xiv, *xvi–xvii*, 1–2, 4–5, 7–9, 11,
    13, 15, 23, 26–33, 36–9, 41–5, 48,
    53, 57–8, 60–2, 64–71, 75, 78–82,
    84, 86–92, 94–6, 98–9, 105, 109,
    112–13, 116, 119–21, 123–5, 129,
    131, 133, 137–51
Drewry, George T., *xviii*, 119, 137,
    147–9
Drewry, Harry Kendall, 12, 106–11,
    125, 131
Drewry, Herbert Percy, 13, 18,
    114–15, 133–6
Drewry, John, 11
Drewry (née Kendall), Mary Ann, 12,
    58, 105, 125, 131
Drewry, Matthew, 12
Drewry, Maud, 131, 133
Drewry, Pleasant, 12
Drewry, Ralph, 13, 15, 17, 72, 114,
    119, 124, 136–7, 147

Drewry Shipping Consultants, 136
Drewry, Thomas, 11–12, 28, 58–9, 70,
    74, 105, 125, 129–31, 133, 148

Emden, Richard van, 89, 93
*Empire of the Deep: The Rise and Fall
    of the British Navy* (book), 21
Epping Forest, 14, 147
Ertugrul Cove, *xi*, 35
Essex County Chronicle (newspaper),
    57

ffoulkes, Maj Charles, 129
Field Ambulance, 89th (1st
    Highland), 5
Fights and Flights (book), 42
Fisher, Adml Jacky, 1
Fleming, Colin, 22
Forest Gate, 13, 57, 114, 123, 147
Forester, C.S., 20, 22
Forshaw VC, William, *xii*
*Four Centuries of Merchant Taylors'
    School* (book), 15
Fraser, John, 27
From Dartmouth to the Dardanelles
    (book), 23–4
Fussell, Prof Paul, *xiv*
Fyffe, PO David, 89

Gallipoli, *xi*, *xvi–xvii*, 2–3, 33, 56–7,
    59–60, 76, 82, 85, 93, 99, 101–102,
    105, 120, 123, 139–41, 144, 148–50
Gallipoli (film), *viii*, *xii*
Gallipoli Memories (book), 93
Gallipoli 1915 (book), 54
Geddes, Capt Guy, 35
Giffard, Capt, 112
Glenparke Road, 11, 13
Globe and Traveller (newspaper),
    60–1
Glory (book), 41

Goodbun, Sub-Lt Alfred Miller, 92, 95
Great Britain's Great War (book), *xiii*
Great War and Modern Memory, The (book), *xiv*
Grimsby, 11–12, 26, 110, 117, 120

Hamilton, Sir Ian, *xvi*, 6, 10, 35, 50, 73–4, 76, 79–80, 82–3, 93–4, 97, 100–102
Hampshires, 2nd, 5, 45, 50, 125
Hampton Road, 15, 13
Hard Lying (book), 3, 33
Hargrave, John, 83, 86
Harris, Clive, *x–xi*, *xviii*, 36, 54, 72
Hart, Peter, *xvii*, 42, 49, 54, 94, 103
Harvey, Maj Francis, 108
Haslam Foundry and Engineering Company, 106
Haslemere (later Kitchener) Road, 53, 13
Heligoland Bight, Battle of, 106
Helles Memorial, *x*
Hell Spit, 90
Herbert, A.P., *xv–xvi*, 51
Hermit Island, 29–30
Hillier, Herbert, *xv*
Hill 141, 46
Hipper, V Adml von, 106
History of the First World War (book), 107
Holland, Skye, *xviii*, 149–51
Holloway, Edgar, 128
Horend, WO William, 5
Hornet, The (comic), 141–2
Hull, 117, 119–20
Hull Daily Mail (newspaper), 57
Humber, the, 11
Hunnisett, Steve, *xviii*, 118–19
Hunter River, 27
Hunter-Weston, Maj Gen Sir Aylmer Gould, 45–6

Imbros, 63, 78, 82–3
Imperial Merchant Service Guild, 73, 125
Imperial War Museum (IWM), 129–30, 138–9, 148, 150
Inchcape, Lord, 74, 129
Indian Mule Corps, 89
Intax Farm, 12, 17
Isaac, Capt Alexander, 28

Jellicoe, Adml Sir John, 6, 106
Joyce, William, 27
Jutland, Battle of, 106–109

Kannengeiser, Col Hans, 38
Keegan, John, 107
Kelly, Dr Peter Burrowes, 5, 7, 44, 48, 70–1, 127, 130
Kemal, Mustafa (later Ataturk), *xii*
Kendall, Drew, 12, 26
Kendall, Eleanor, 26, 110
Kendall, George, 12
Kendall, Naomi, 12
Kendall, Ronald, *xvii*, 111
Kerr, Charles, 5
Kerr, John, 5
Keyes, Cdre (later Adml) Sir Roger, 40–1, 53, 87, 96, 100
King George V, 71–2
Kitchener, FM Lord, 13, 78, 94, 113
Kobe, Japan, 18, 114
Konstam, Angus, 122
Krithia, Second Battle of, 48, 90

Lala Baba, *ix*, 83, 86
Lancashire Fusiliers, *xi*, 84
Leaf, Walter, 55
Lemnos, 3, 82
Liddell Hart, Basil, 107, 109
London Gazette, The (newspaper), 52, 73
Lord Ashcroft Gallery, 138

Mackenzie, Compton, *xv*, 93
Mahmut, Maj, 42
Maidos (Eceabat), 82
Malleson VC, Wilfred St Aubyn, 43–4, 60, 64, 140
Malta, 32, 112, 140
Manchesters, 11th, *viii–x*
Manchester, Sheffield and Lincolnshire Railway Company, 11
Mantel, Hilary, *xiv*
Marryat, Capt Frederick, *xiv*, 20, 22, 59, 61
Masefield, John, *xv*, 36, 75, 93, 148
Melbourne Argus (newspaper), 1, 141
Merchant Taylors' School, 15–16, 58, 137–8
Meugens, Capt Geoffrey, 84
Military History Monthly (magazine), 54
Mr Midshipman Easy (book), *xiv*, 11, 23, 52
Mitylene, 82
Moorehead, Alan, 65, 102
Moran, Francis, 28
Morrow, Canon, 123–4
Morse DSO, Lt John Anthony 'Tony' Vere, 43
Morto Bay, 50
Mount, The, 17
Moynihan, Michael, 17, 72, 137
Mudros, 2–4, 8, 77, 112
Munro, Sir Charles, 100
Mure TD, Maj A.H., 19, 50–1
Murray, OS Joe, 101

Nairn, John Arbuthnot, 15–16
Napier, Brig Gen Henry Edward, 45
Nation, The (magazine), 62
Newcastle, New South Wales, 27
Newham, 141
News of the World, The (newspaper), 6
Nibrunesi Point, 80–1, 86

Northern Patrol, 119–20, 125
North Staffordshire Blind and Deaf School, 18
Northumberland Fusiliers, *x*

O'Brian, Patrick, 20,
O'Brien, Capt R. Barry, 140
Orcadian, The (newspaper), 121
Orkneys, *xiii*, 113, 119, 121–2
Ottoman Empire, xi, 2, 23, 25, 42, 54, 77, 82
Ouse, River, 117–18

Paxman, Jeremy, *xiii*
Peninsular & Orient Steamship Company (P&O), 7, 12, 14, 18, 31, 47, 74, 106, 114, 129–30
Pepys, Samuel, 19
Port Said, 1, 31–2, 105, 112, 143
Place Called Armageddon, A (book), 137
Portsmouth Evening News (newspaper), 140
Preston, E. Carter, 125
Price, Midshipman James, 79
Punch (magazine), 63

Quiet Shore, The (book,) *xvi*, 142

Rainscombe Park, 135
Raymond, Ernest, *xv–xvi*, 85, 139
Reeman, Douglas (*aka* Alexander Kent), *xv*, 20, 22, 33, 40
Reith Lectures, *xiv*
Robeck, V Adml John de, 8, 52, 57, 59, 66, 74, 83
Romford Road, 13–14, 17
Rosyth, 106, 108–10
Royal Albert Docks, 13–14, 130
Royal Army Medical Corps, *xiii*, 5
Royal Dublin Fusiliers, 1st, 5, 36, 50, 125

Royal Humane Society, 28
Royal Munster Fusiliers, 1st, 5, 35–6, 50, 125
Royal Naval Armoured Car Squadron, 5, 89
Royal Naval College, Osborne, 23–4, 71
Royal Naval Division Anson Battalion, 5
Royal Naval Reserve, *xi*, *xv*, 31–2, 64, 73, 147
Russell, Midshipman Greg, 64

Samson, Air Cdre Charles Rumney, 42
Samson, Seaman George 'Geordie', 2, 5, 39, 46, 49, 53, 67–72, 125, 139
Sanders, Gen Liman von, 38
Sarajevo, 18
Sari Bair, 80
Sassoon, 2nd Lt Hamo Watts, 101
Sassoon, Siegfried, xv, 102
Scapa Flow, *xiii*, 6, 106, 110, 112–13, 119–20, 122
Scheer, Adml, 106, 110
Sedd-el-Bahr, *xi*, 35–6, 42, 46, 48, 55
Secret Battle, The (book), *xvi*, 51
Selby, 117–19
Seldon, Anthony, 105
Shaw-Stewart, Patrick, *xv*, 18
Sheffield, Prof Gary, 56
Ships,
  Agamemnon, 24–5
  Albion, 34–5
  Arcadian, 3
  Bacchante, 97
  Bouvet, 25,
  Chester, 109
  Conqueror, 112–13, 122
  Cornwallis, 43,
  Dundrennan, 88, 97
  Egmont, 32

Endymion, 78
Europa, 92
Euryalus, 66
Fauvette, 9
Glory, 81–2
Goliath, 23
Hampshire, 113, 122
Hussar, 2, 4–5, 32–3, 46, 67, 71, 77, 98, 101, 105, 113, 143
Hythe, 71
Ikalis, 98
Implacable, 120
Indefatigible, 107
Indian Empire, 26–30, 92
Inflexible, 92
Irresistible, 25
Isis, 31–2
Jervis Bay, 136
Jonquil, 83, 86, 88, 94, 97
Kildonan Castle, 101
Lancastria, 134
Lion, 108
Lützow, 108
Markgraf, 109
Minneapolis, 88
Moltke, 107
Monarch, 112
Nusret, 25
Ocean, 25, 79
Palma, 31
Prince George, 88
Princess Royal, 105, 107–10
Queen Elizabeth, 144
Queen Mary, 107–108
Ramazan, 88–9, 91, 95–6
Reliance, 4
River Clyde / Marija y Aurora, 2, 4, 8–10, 35–54, 56, 58, 71, 112, 125–6, 128, 137, 139, 143–9
Sarnia, 71
Soudan, 9, 97
Spiraea, 111

Swiftsure, 97–9
Titanic, 30
Triad, 52
Vanguard, 113, 122
William Jackson / Lord Byng / Evelyn Rose, 116–21, 123, 126, 149
Sillery, Lt Col Charles, *x*
Sillery, Maj John 'Jack', viii–x, 84–5
Sims VC, John Joseph, 124
Snelling, Stephen, *xvii*, 9, 39, 44, 48
Social History of Midshipmen, A (book), 19
Somme, The, *x*, 64, 93
Song of Roland, The (poem), *xv*
Spenser, Edmund, 16, 137
Steel, Nigel, *xvii*, 36, 39, 49, 149
Stokes, Dennis 'Denny', 138
Stopford, Lt Gen Sir Frederick, 83, 93–4
Stratford Express, The (newspaper), 123, 130
Sudan, 5, 83
Sunday Post (newspaper), 67
Suvla Bay, *ix*, *xiv*, 63, 74–5, 77, 83, 85–6, 89, 91, 98–101, 103
Suvla Bay Landing, The (book), 86
Suvla Point, 80–1, 88

Tatler (magazine), 63
Tell England (book), *xvi*
Tell England (film), 139–40
Tenedos, 8–9
Thorne, Heather, *xvii*
Tilbury, 12
Times, The (newspaper), 55–7, 76–7, 100–101
Tisdall VC, Sub Lt Arthur 'Pog', 5, 45, 125
Tizard, Lt Colonel Henry, 40
Towler and Son, 136
Troy (film), *x*
Truth (magazine), 62–3

Uncensored Dardanelles (book), *xiii*
Unwin, Cdr (later Capt) Edward, 2–10, 33, 36, 38–41, 44–5, 48–50, 53, 58, 65–70, 72, 77, 87–8, 98, 100, 112, 139, 145

V Beach, *xi*, *xiv*, 3, 36, 42, 45–6, 48–50, 52, 56, 58, 66, 77, 80, 125, 128, 137–9, 148
Victoria Cross, *xi–xii*, 7, 15, 53, 57–9, 62, 64, 72, 74, 77, 99, 121, 125, 127–8, 133, 140–1, 147–8, 150

W Beach, *xi*, 3, 52
Wales, Sir Robin, 141
Walford VC, Capt Garth Neville, 64
Wanstead Park, 17
Ward, Capt George Perkins, 26, 28, 57–8
Water Lane Board School, 17
Wedgwood DSO, Lt Col (later the Baron) Josiah, 5, 7, 34, 48
Weir, Peter, *viii*, *xii*
Weld Forester, Wolstan Beaumont Charles, 23–4
Weldon MC, Capt L.B., 3, 33
Welholme Road, Grimsby, 12, 17
Wemyss, R Adml (later Lord Wester-Wemyss) Rosslyn 'Rosy', 3, 6, 33, 47, 49, 65, 87, 102
Western Evening Herald (newspaper), 58
West Ham Technical Institute, 15
West Riding Field Company, 1st, 5, 125
Whelan, Michael J., *xv*, 116
Wilkinson, Norman, *xv*, 73, 80–1, 94
Williams, Lt Col (later Maj Gen) Weir de Lancey, 5, 37
Williams VC, Seaman William, 5, 39, 41, 53, 72, 139
Wilson, Ben, 21

With Machine Guns at Gallipoli (book), 7

Wooden Horse of Gallipoli, The (book), xvii

X Beach, 3

Y Beach, 3, 90

Ypres, Second Battle of, 2